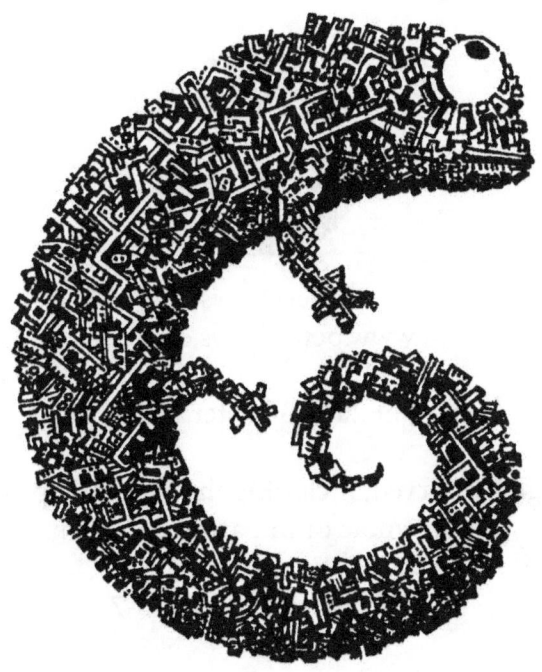

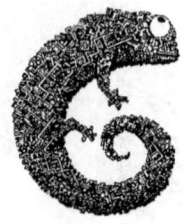

PeterDraws
www.peterdraws.com

Copyright 2013 by Peter Deligdisch

ISBN: 978-1-490-40566-7

To all my fans and supporters both on and offline

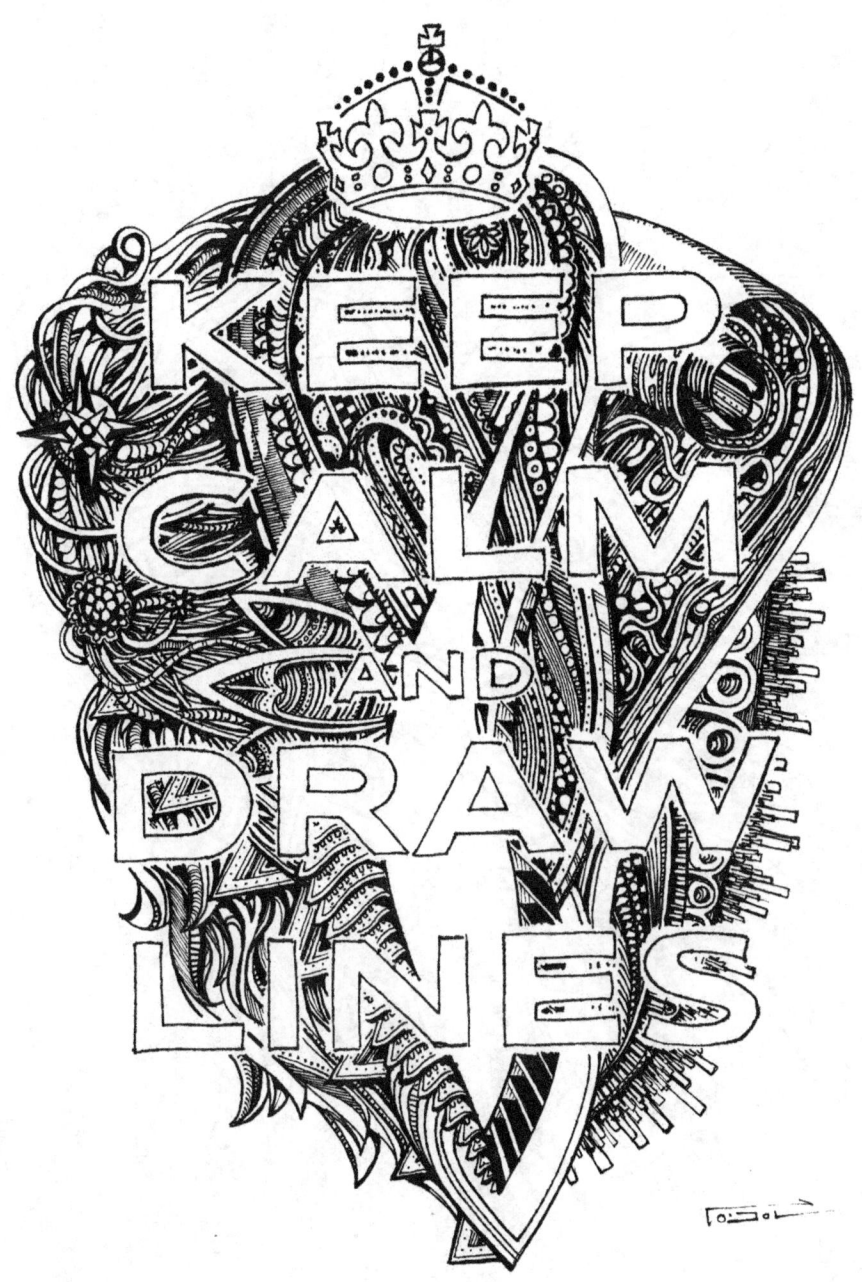

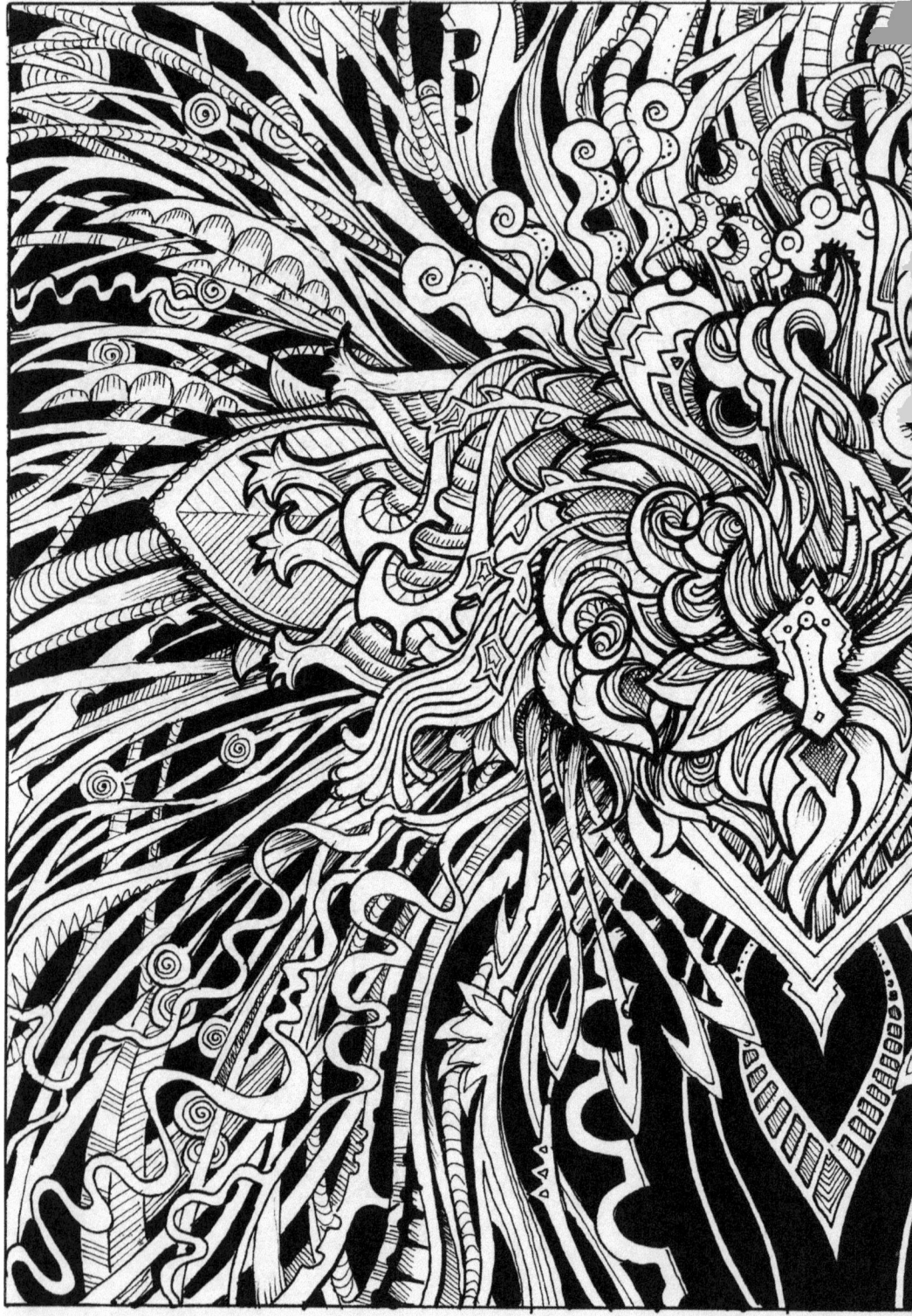

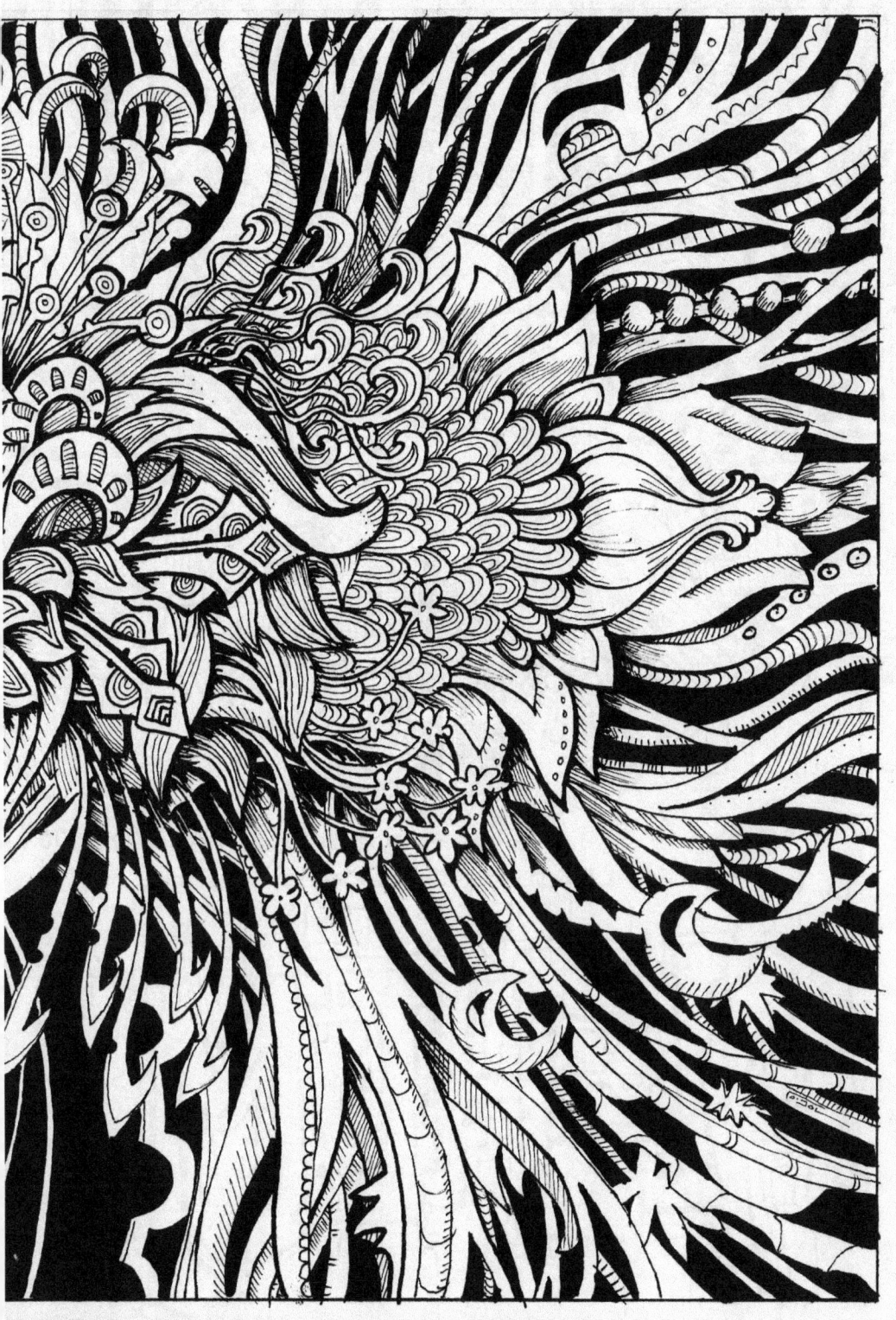

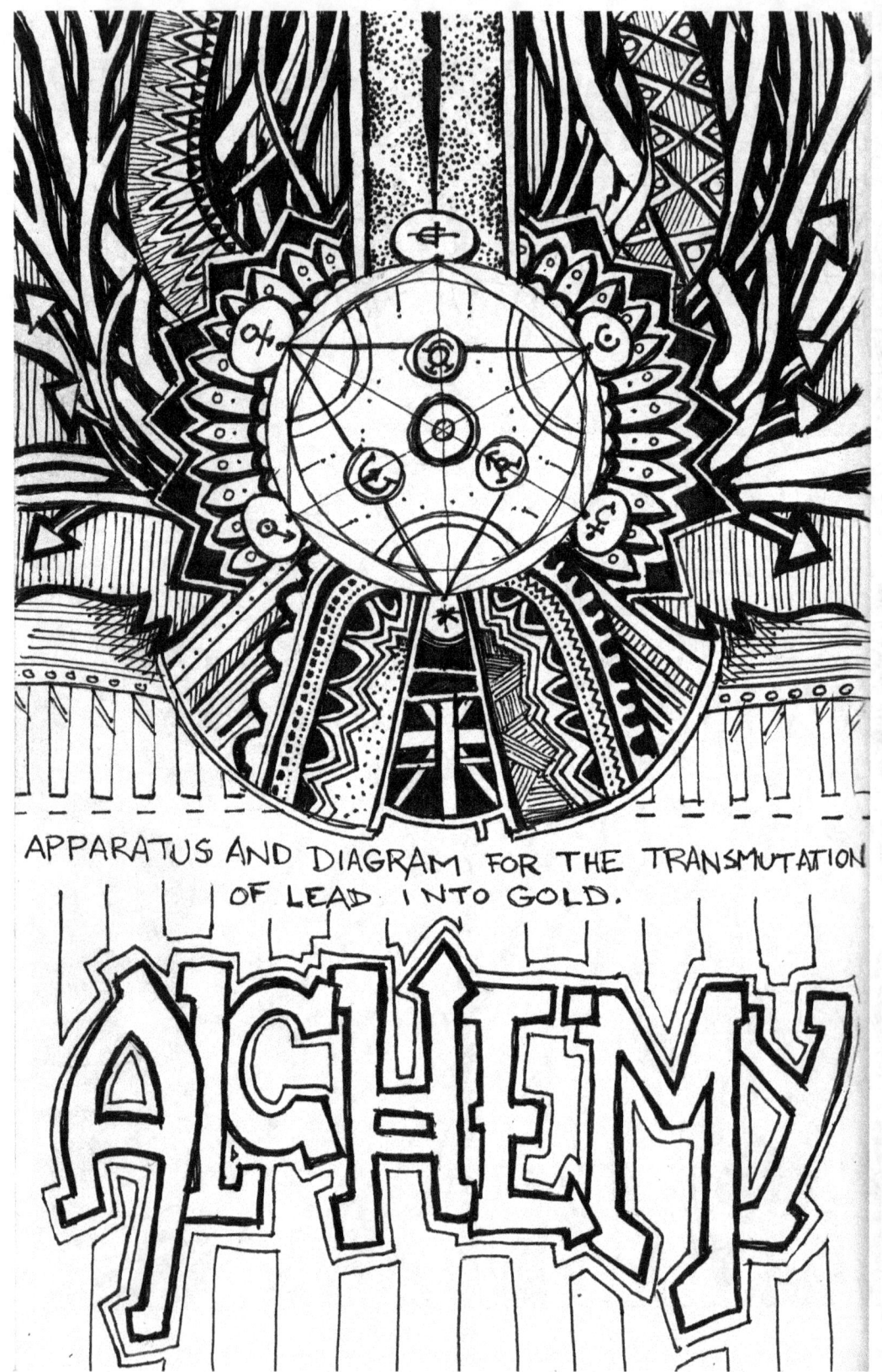

APPARATUS AND DIAGRAM FOR THE TRANSMUTATION OF LEAD INTO GOLD.

ALCHEMY

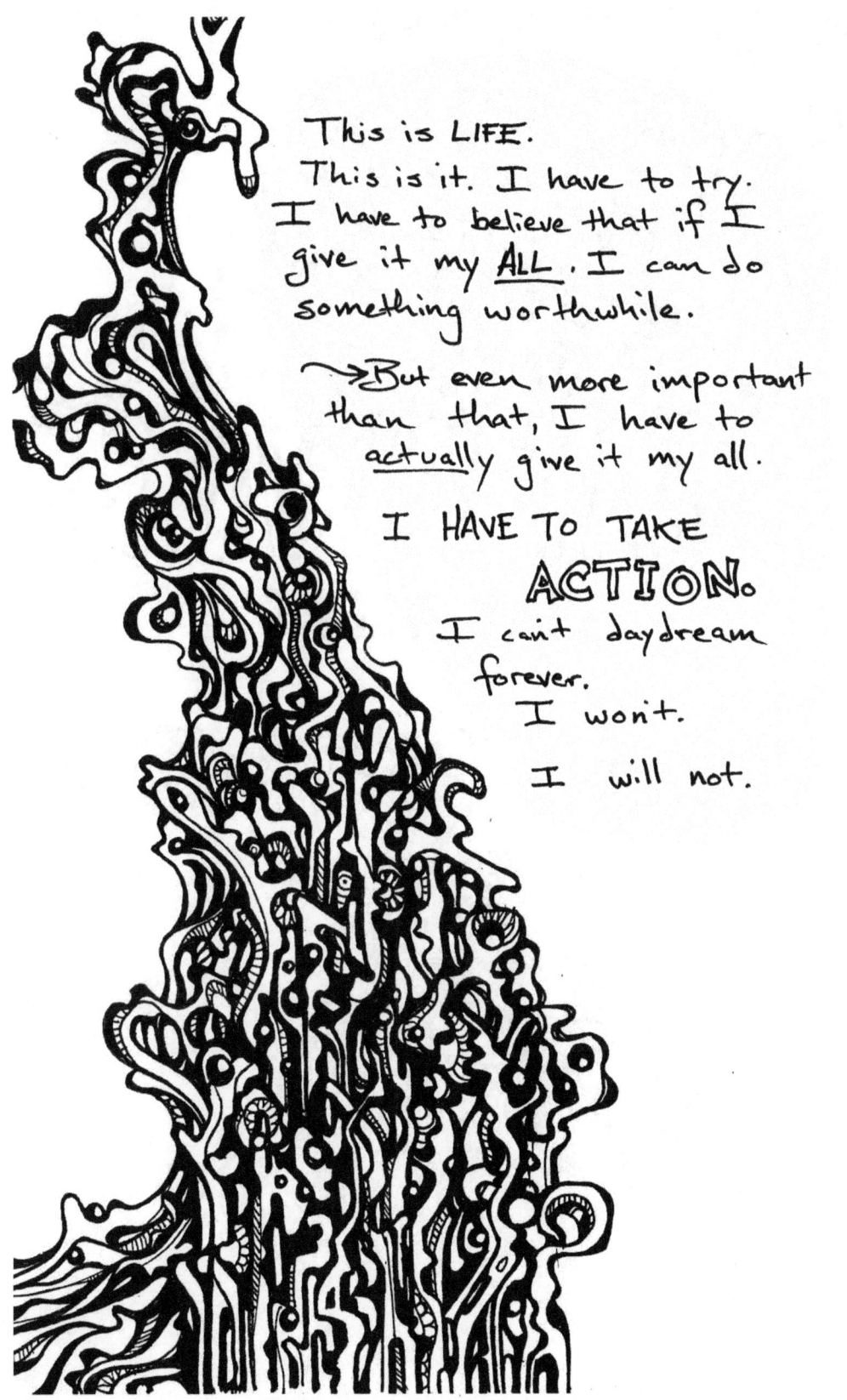

This is LIFE.
This is it. I have to try.
I have to believe that if I
give it my ALL, I can do
something worthwhile.

→But even more important
than that, I have to
actually give it my all.

I HAVE TO TAKE
ACTION.
I can't daydream
forever.
I won't.

I will not.

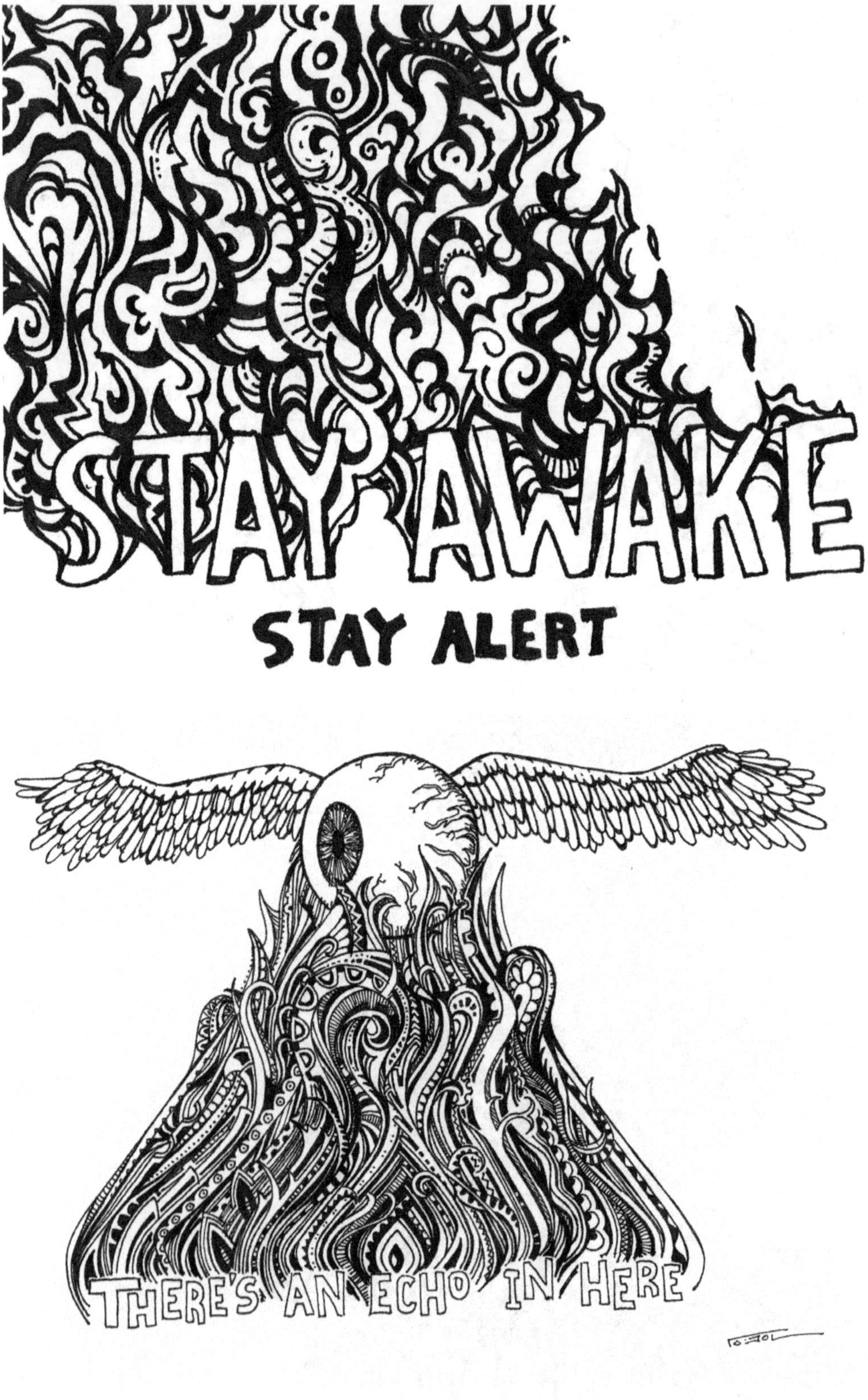

STAY AWAKE
STAY ALERT

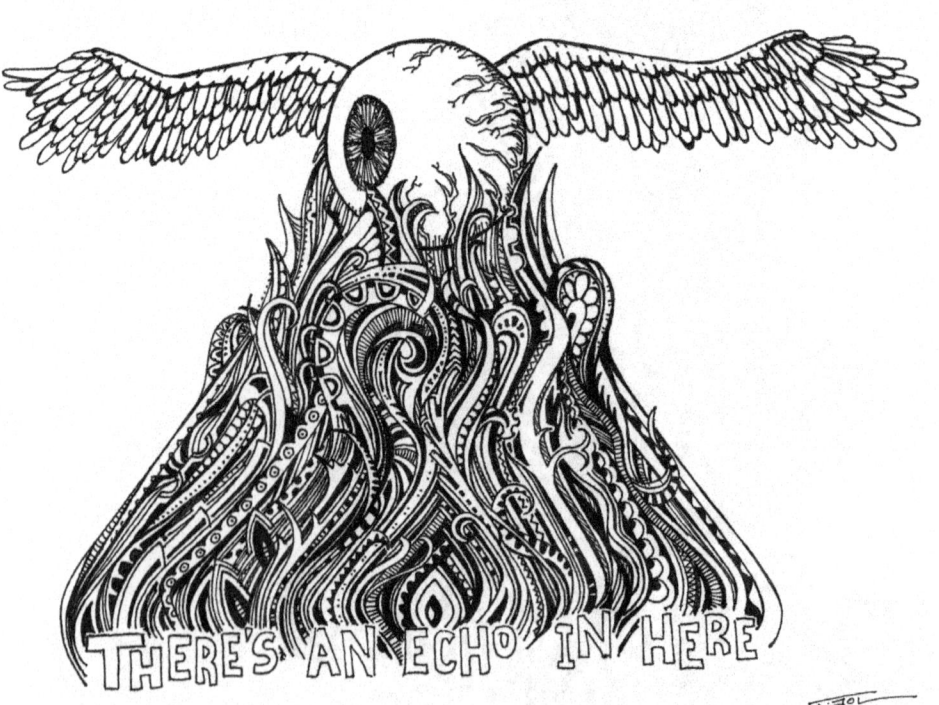

THERE'S AN ECHO IN HERE

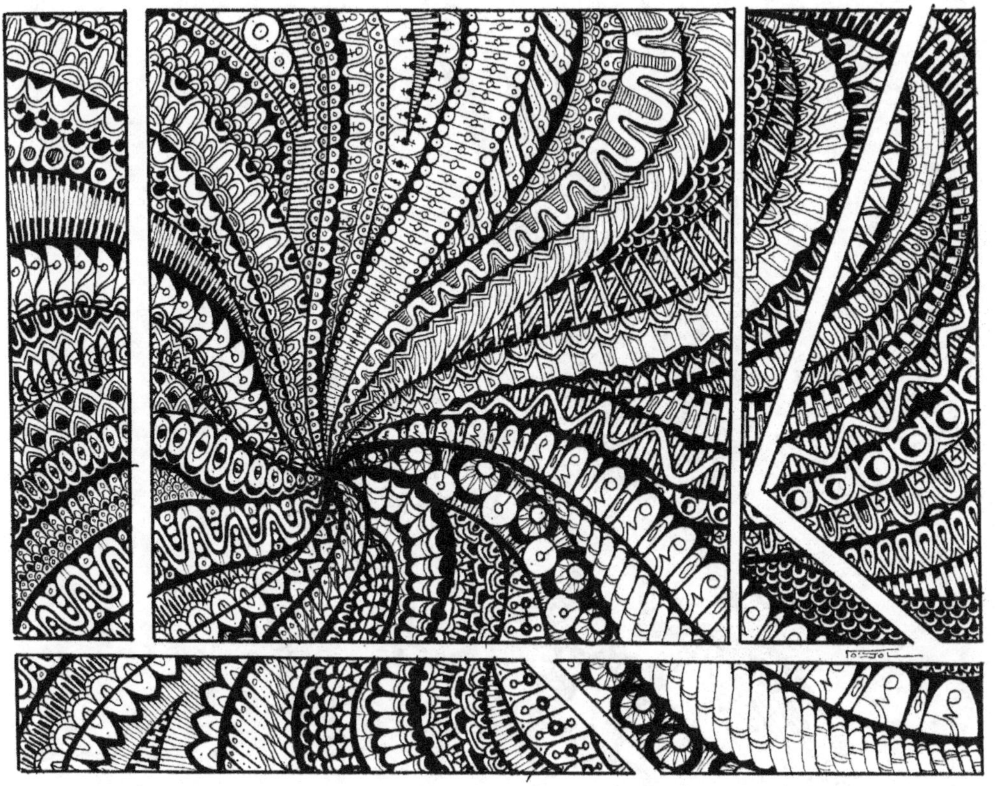

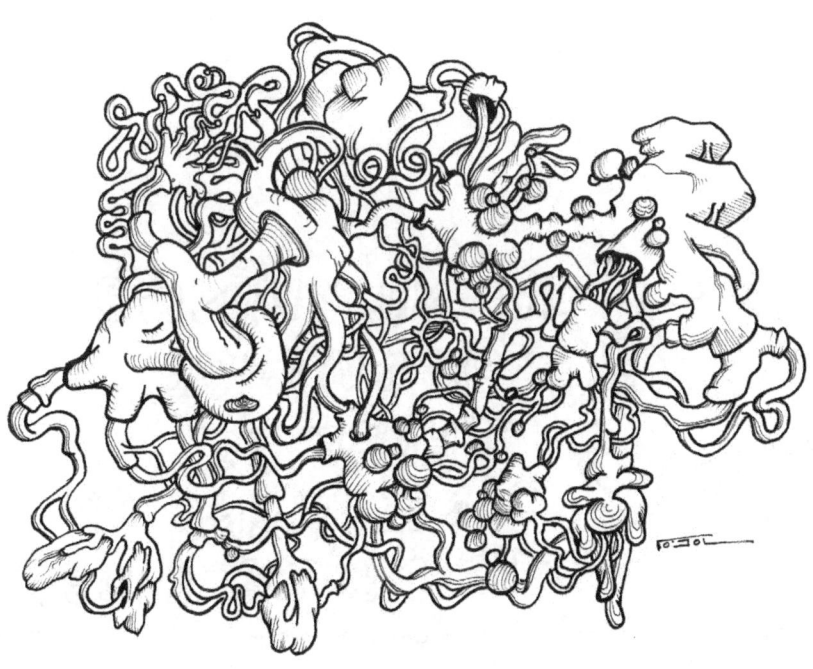

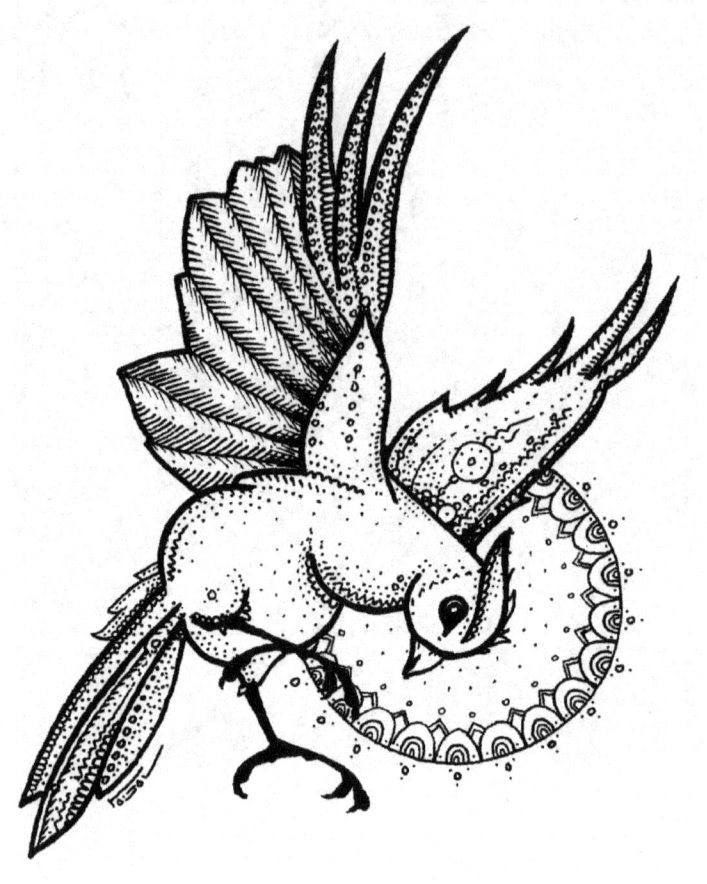

IN ALL THINGS
OF NATURE
THERE IS
SOMETHING OF
THE MARVELOUS.

-ARISTOTLE

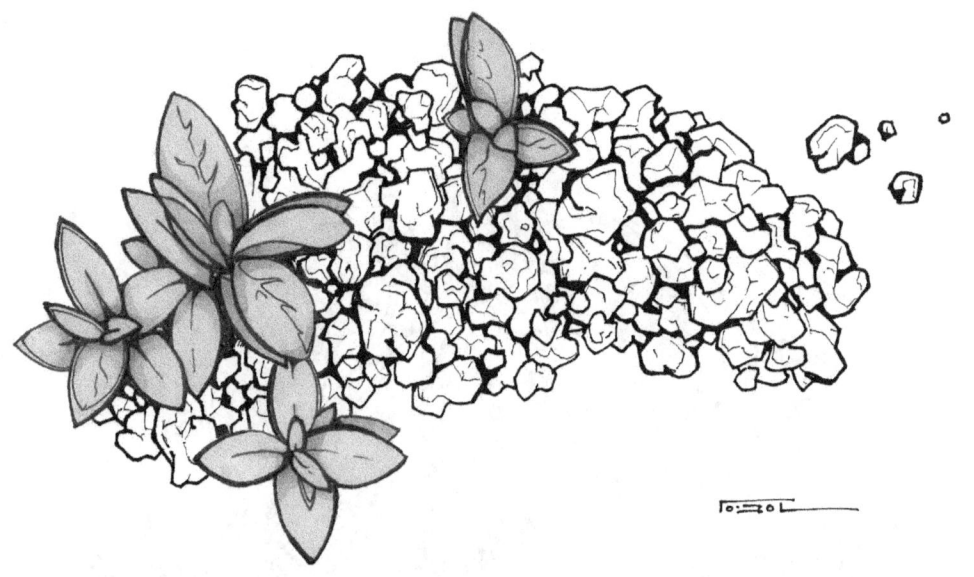

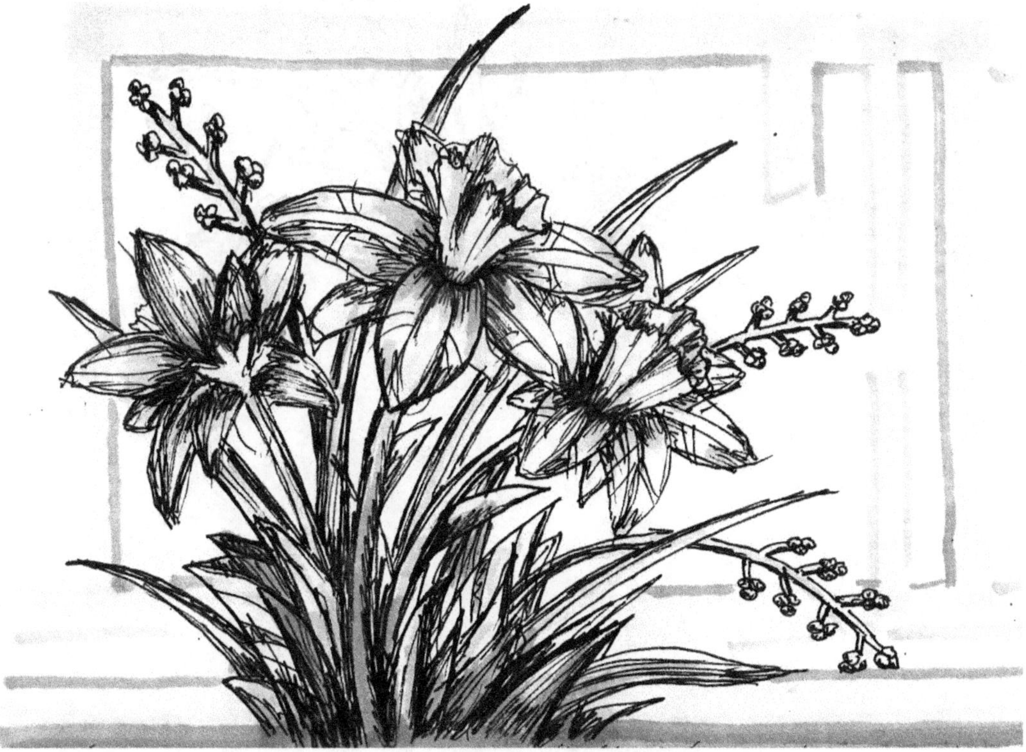

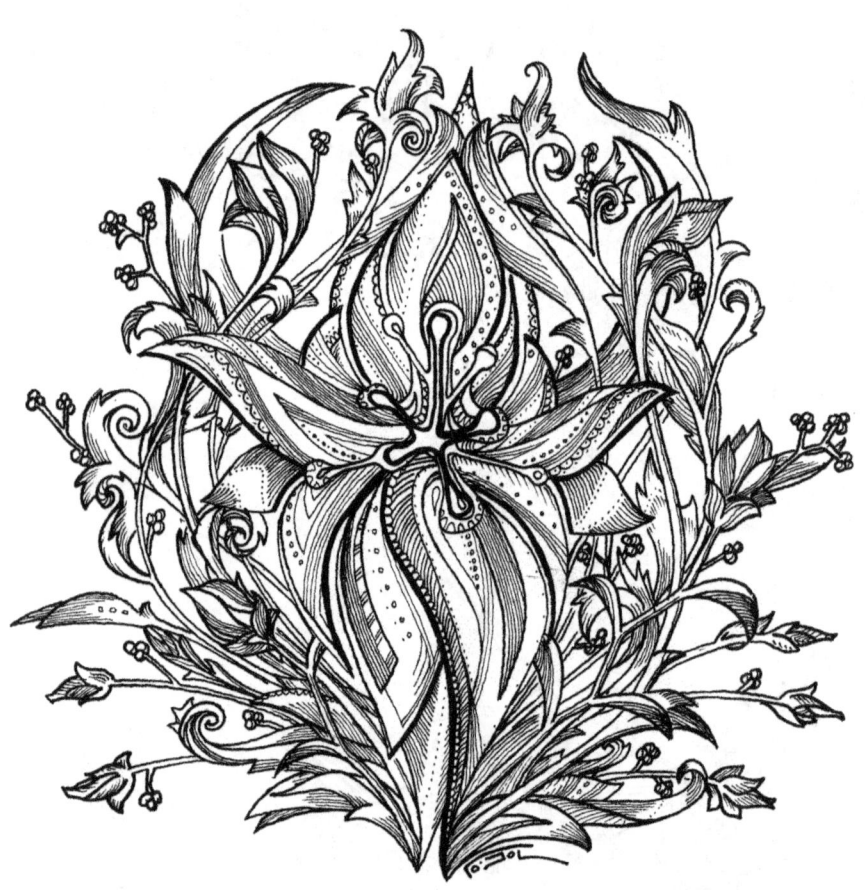

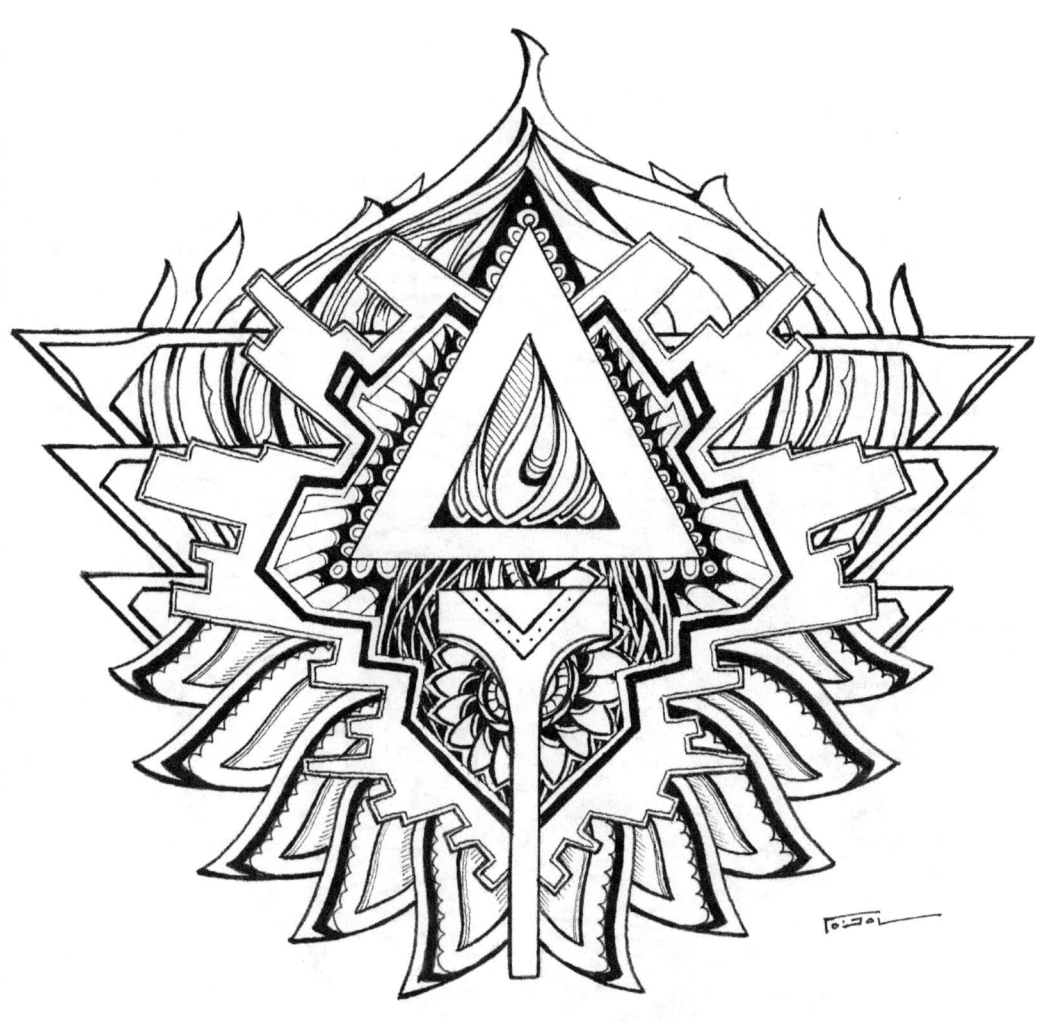

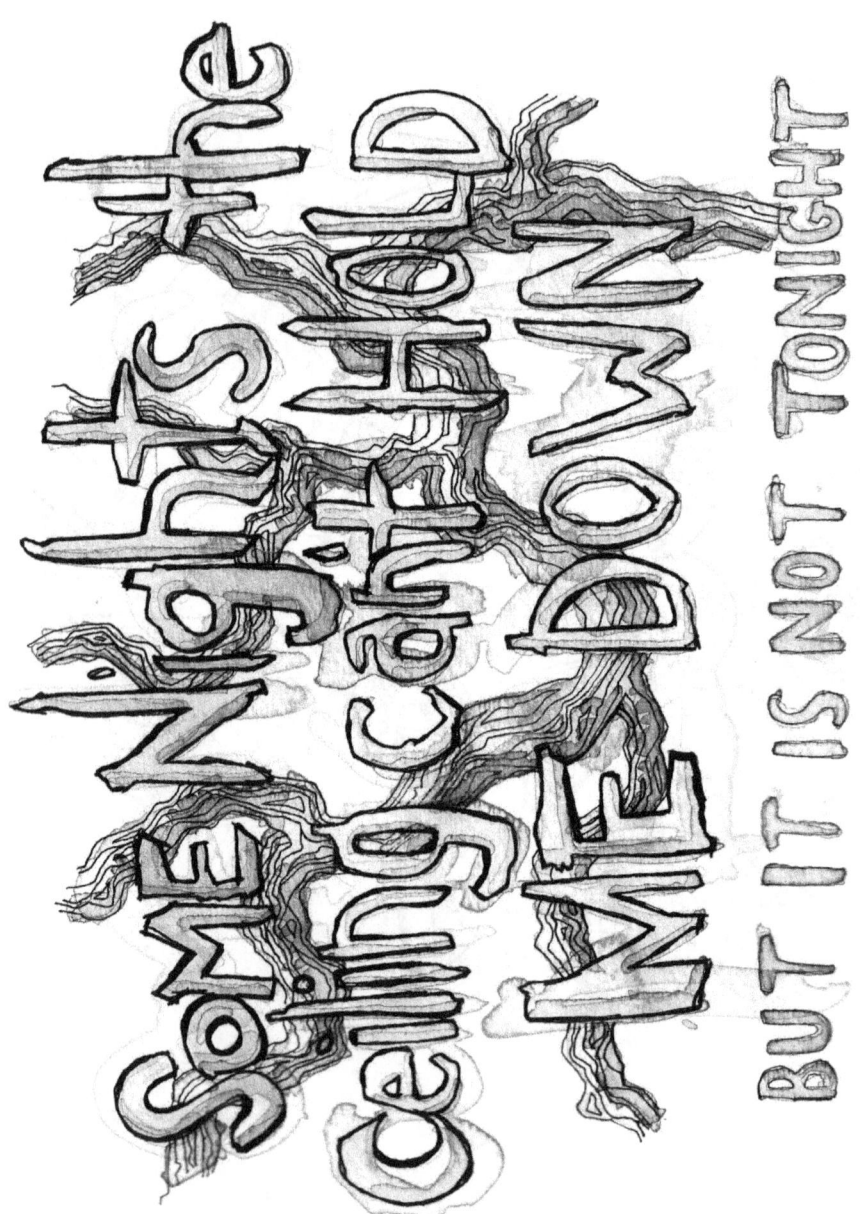

BUT IT IS NOT TONIGHT

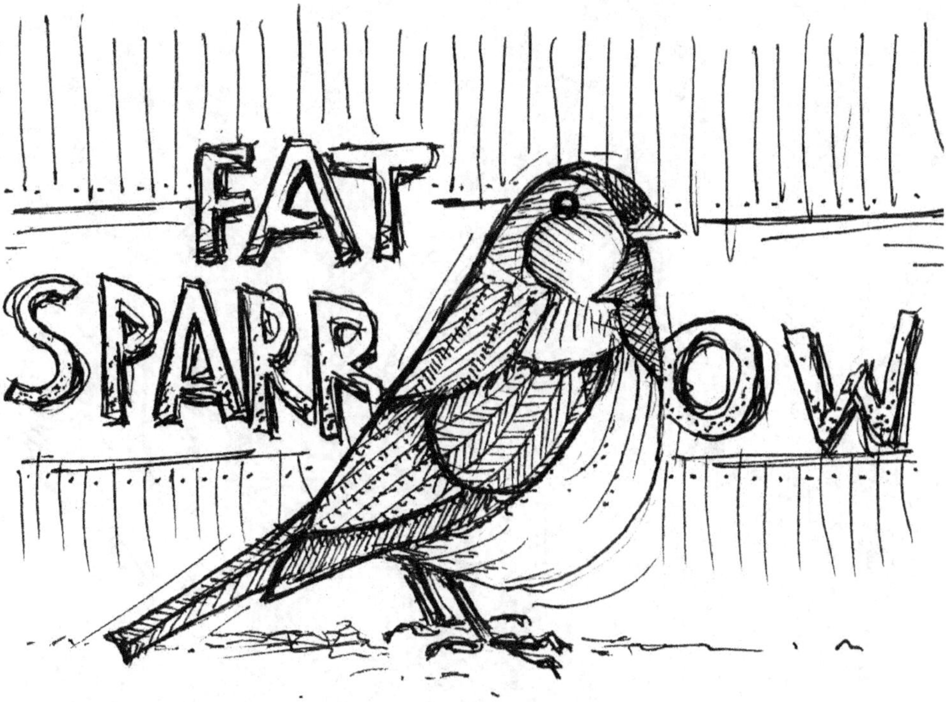
FAT
SPARROW

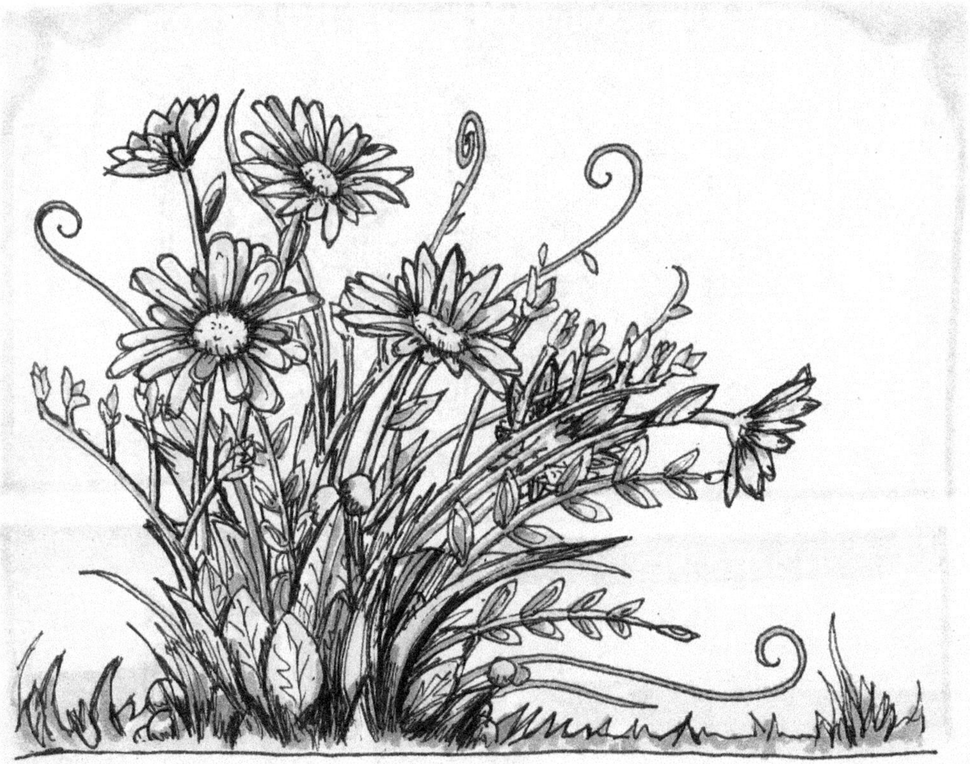

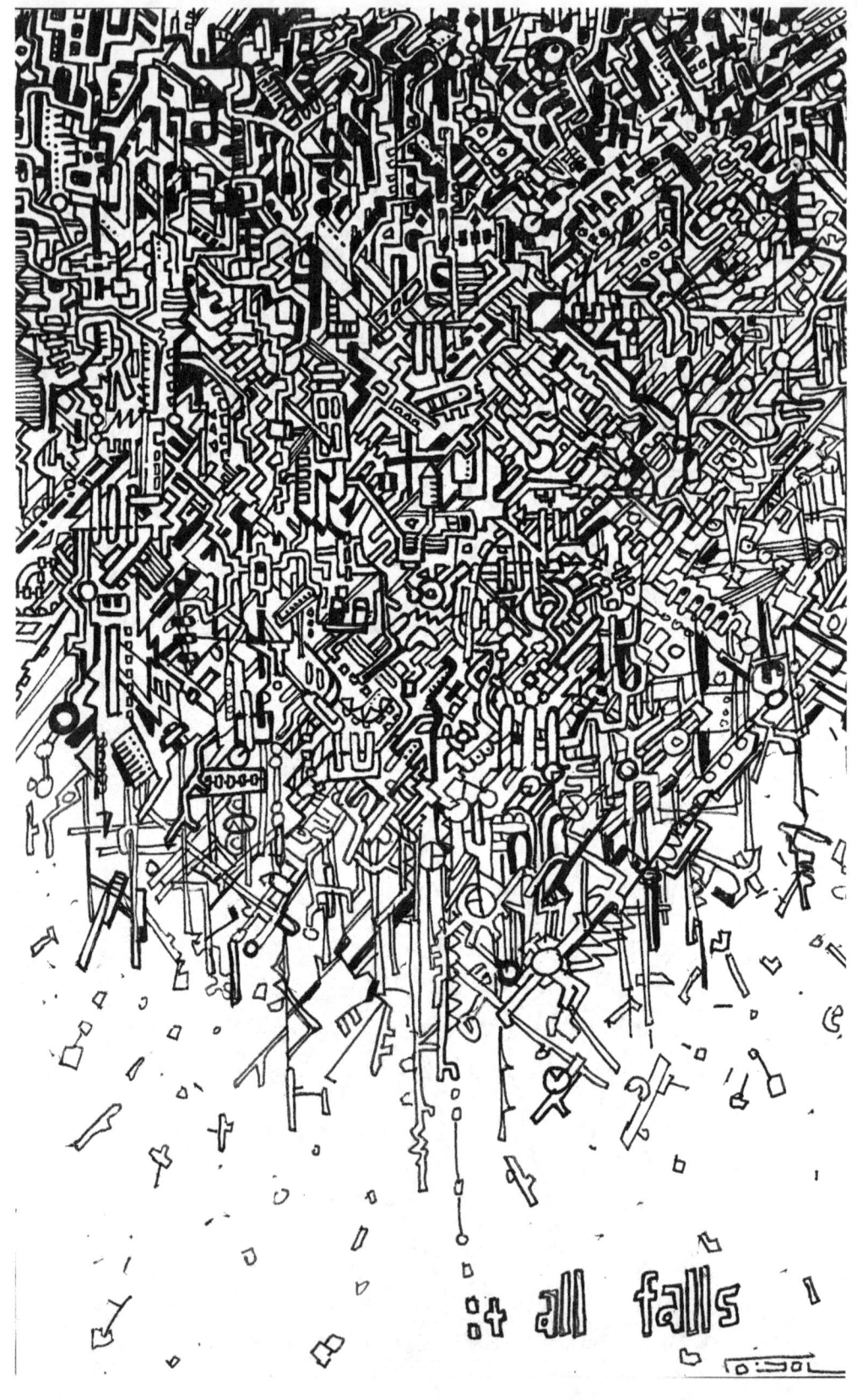

it all falls

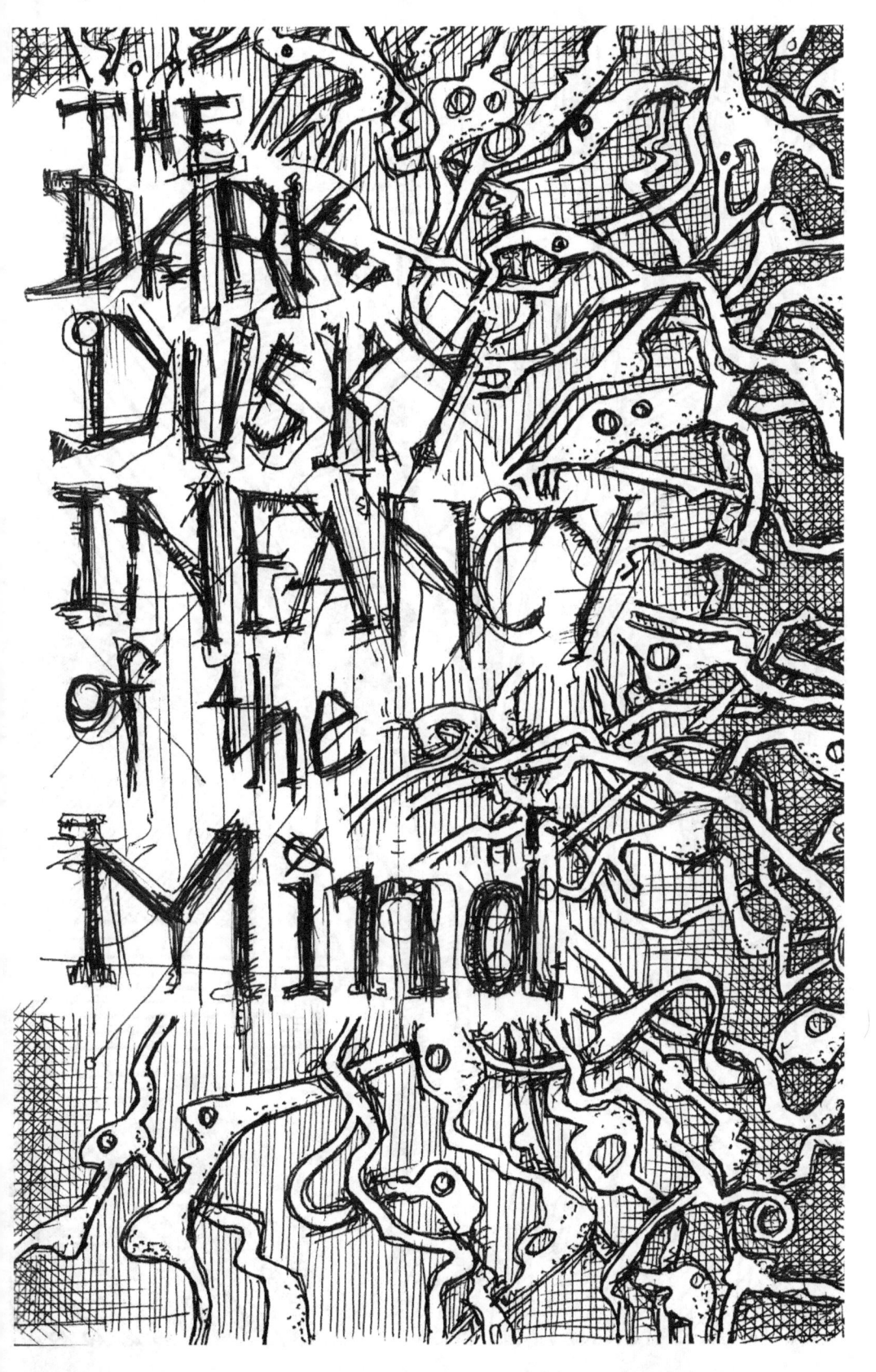

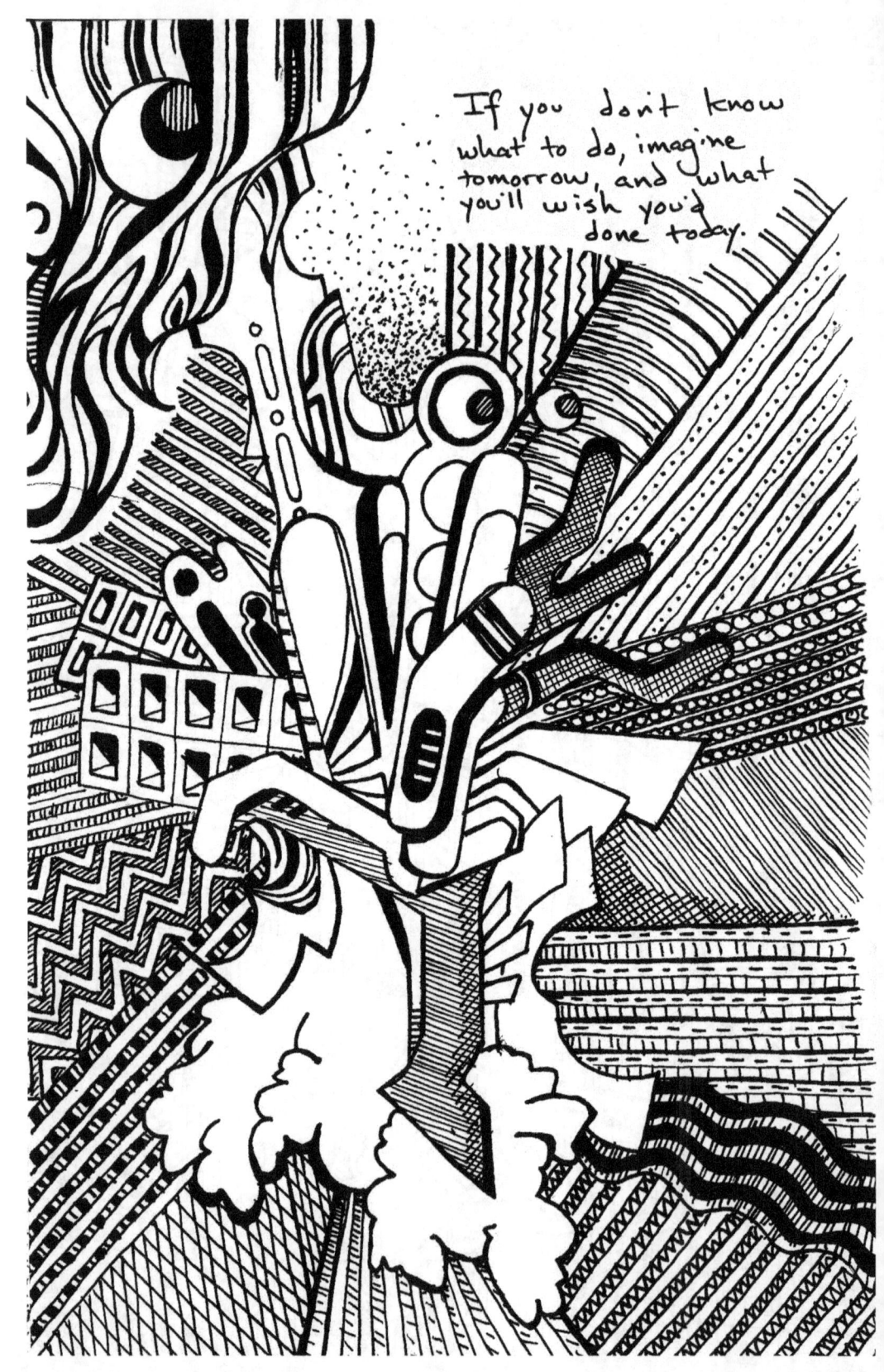

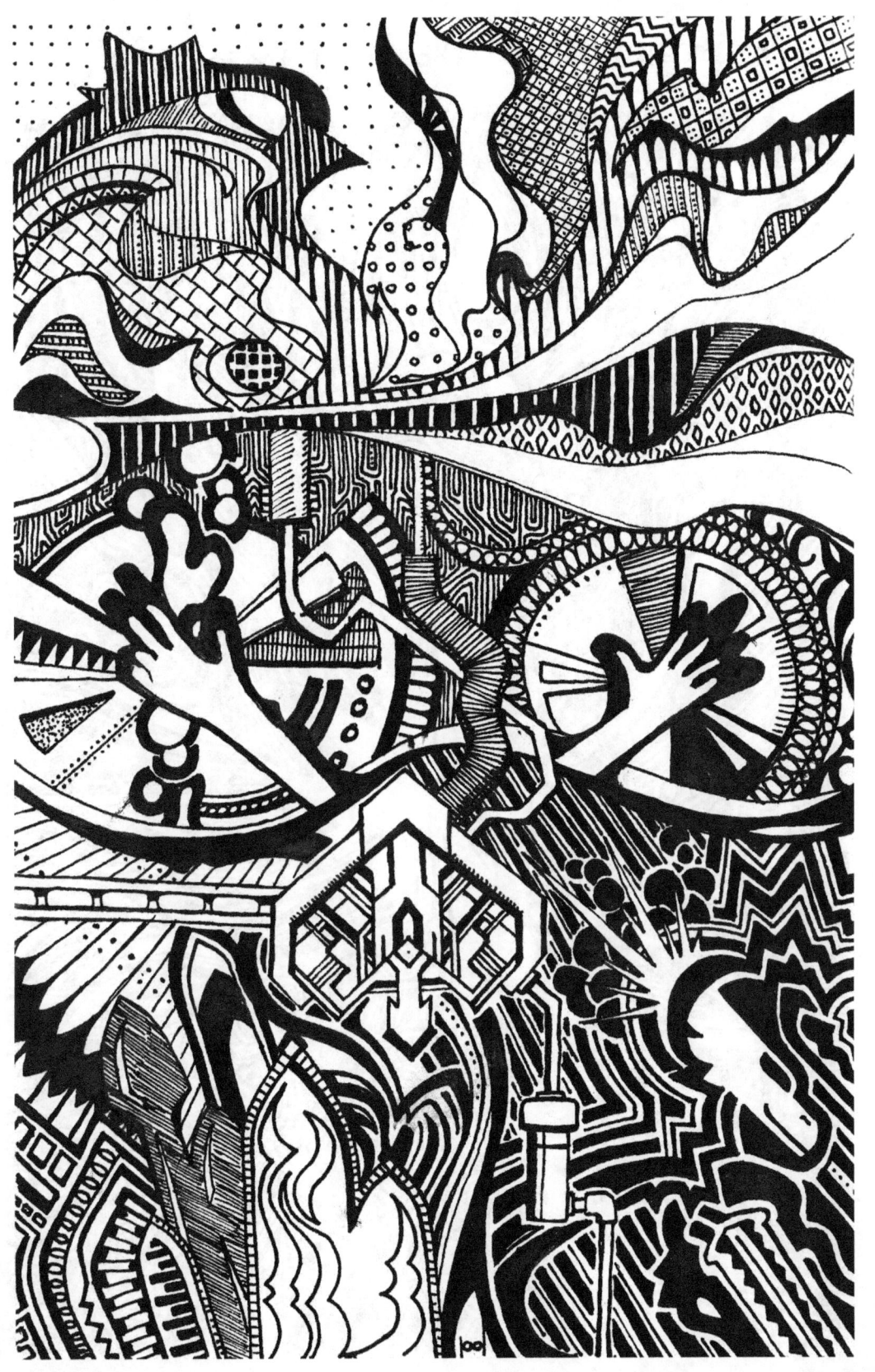

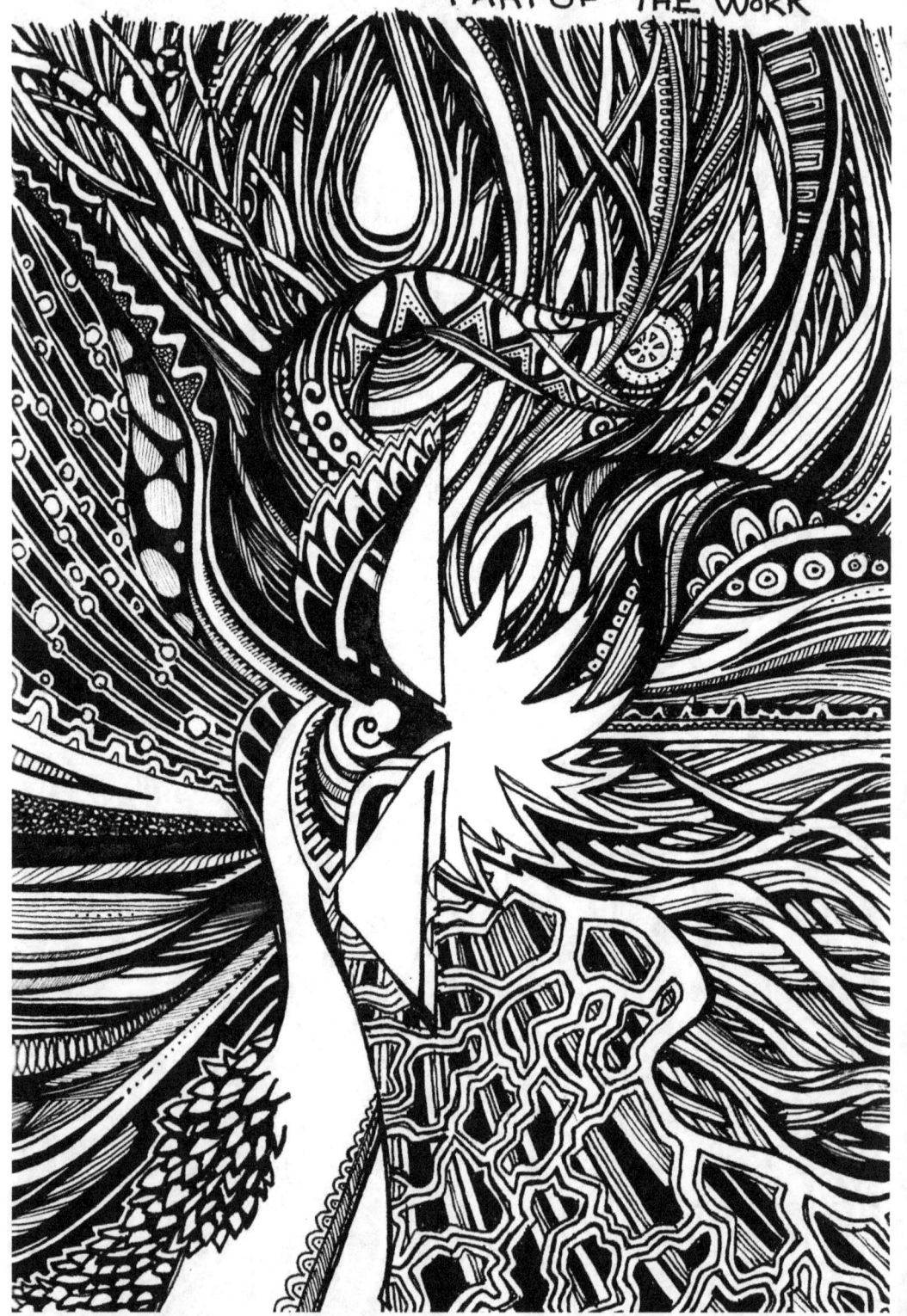

I know there have to be things I haven't thought of yet. That bothers me, so I try to think more, of new things. Of different things. It is a daunting task.
To find the thoughts evading you.

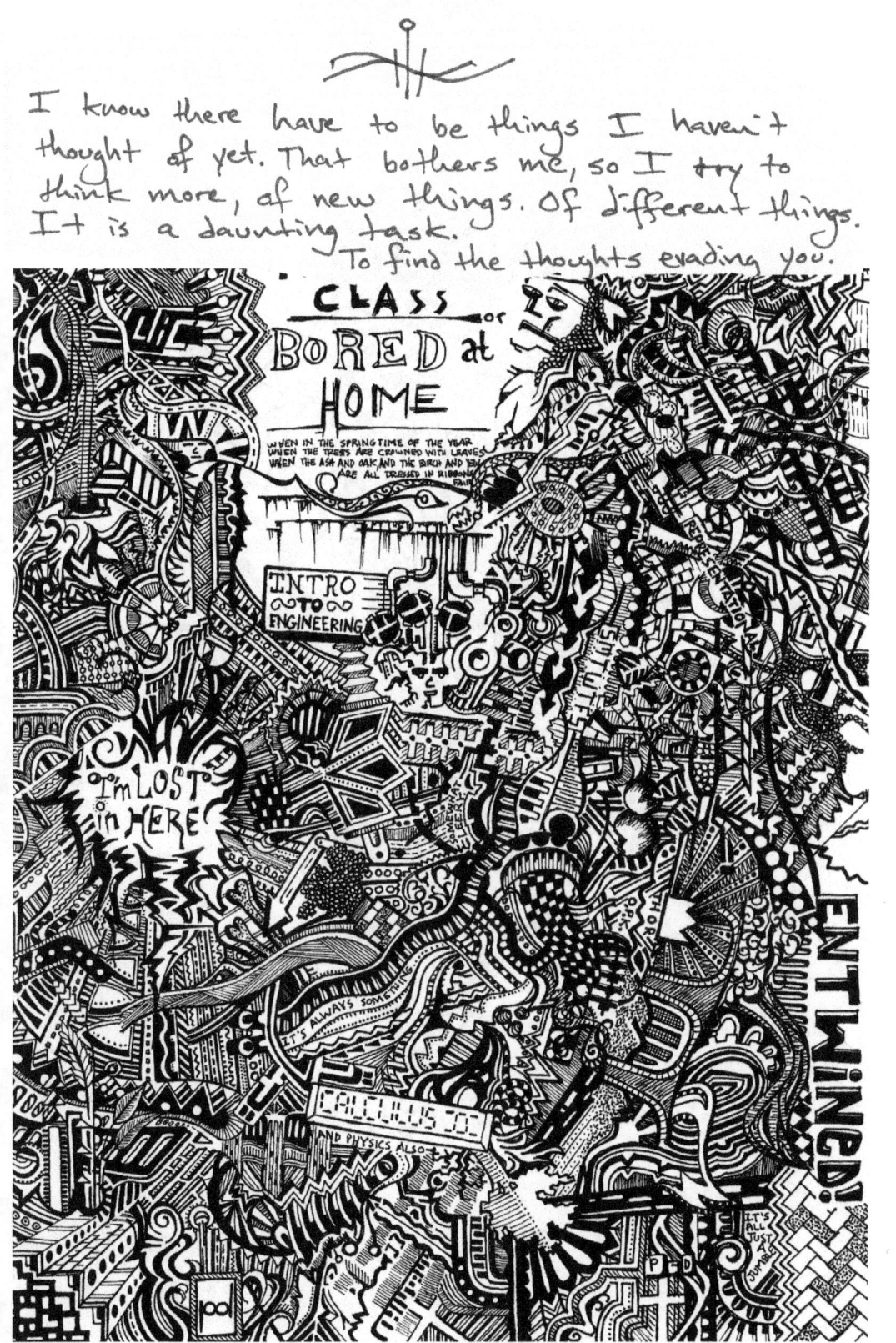

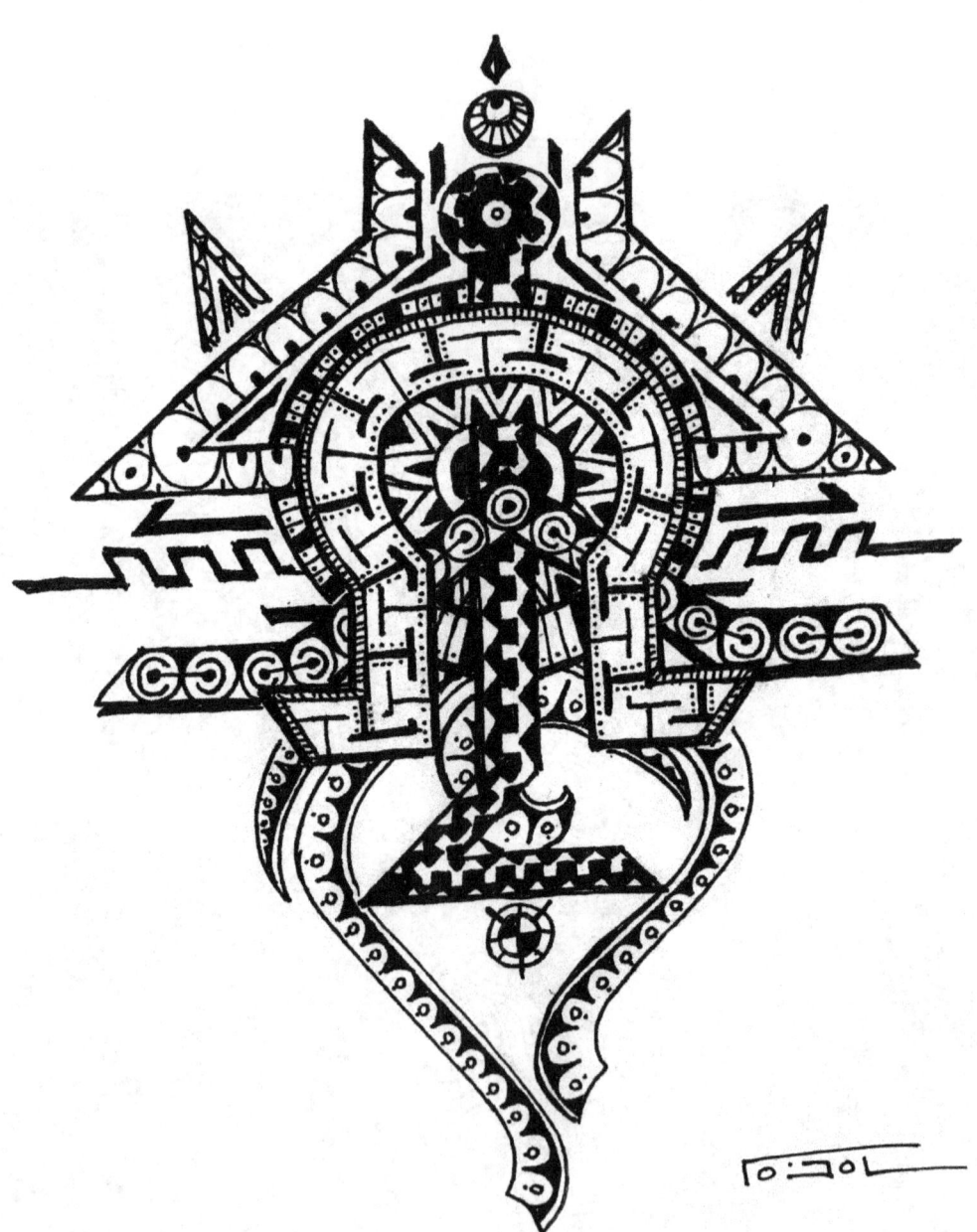

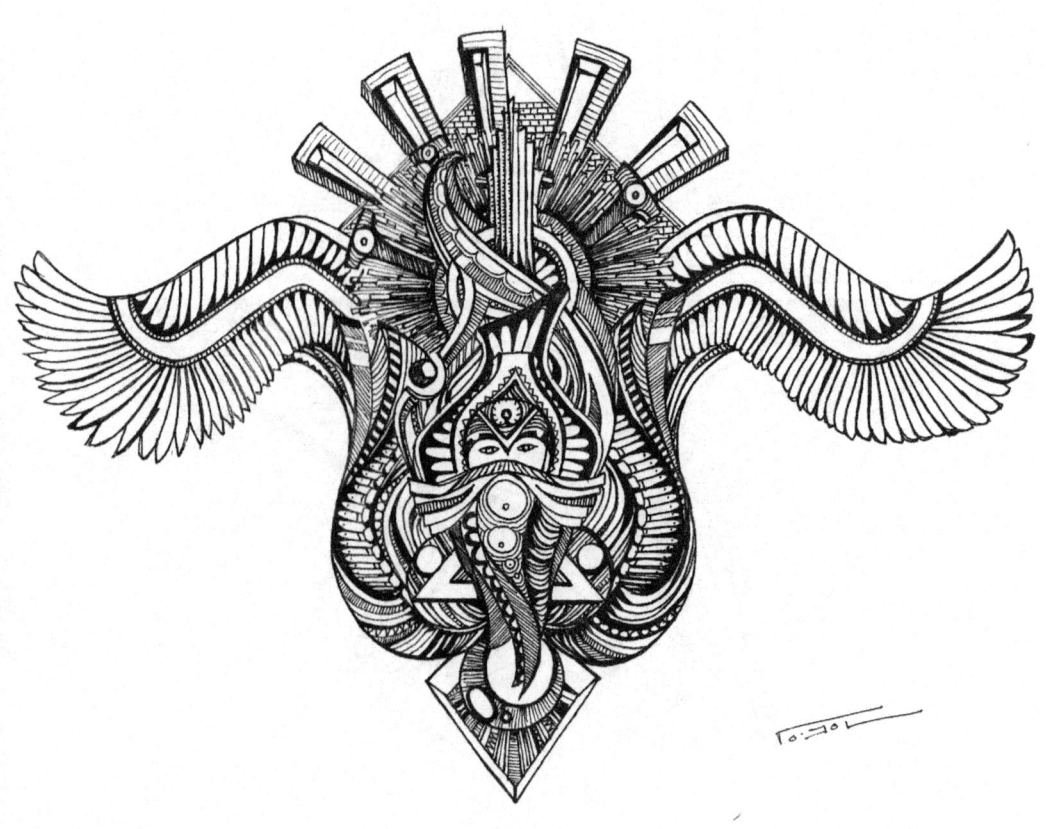

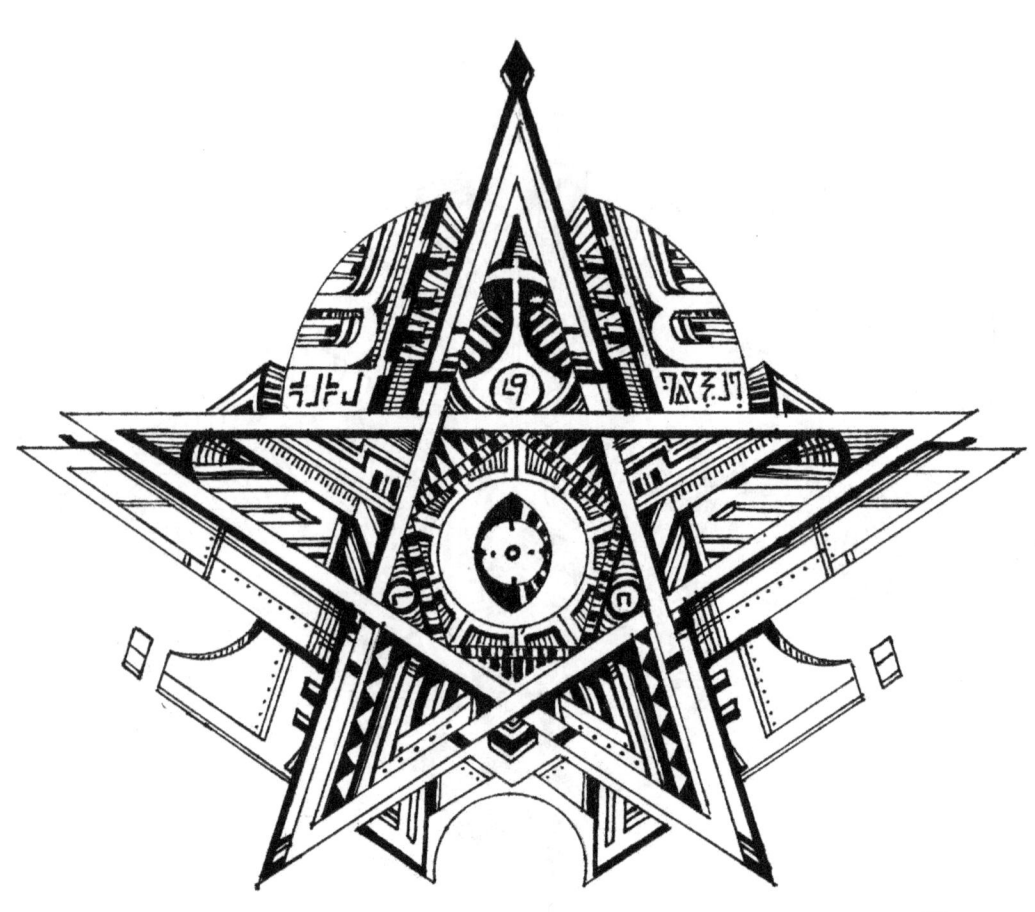

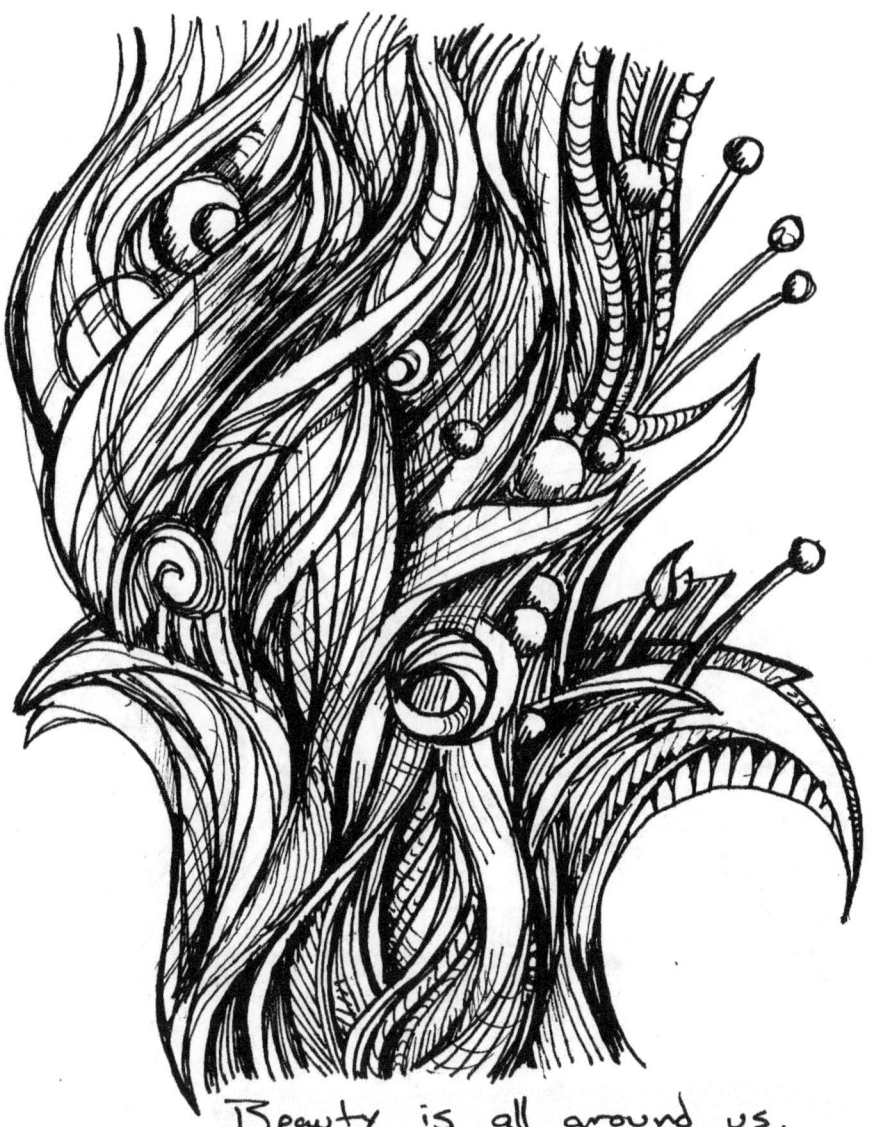

Beauty is all around us.
I know it sounds cliché, but
it's true. If I can't find something
inspiring, I have no one to blame but
myself. It is my fault that I am
not observant enough to call forth the
riches of the world around me.

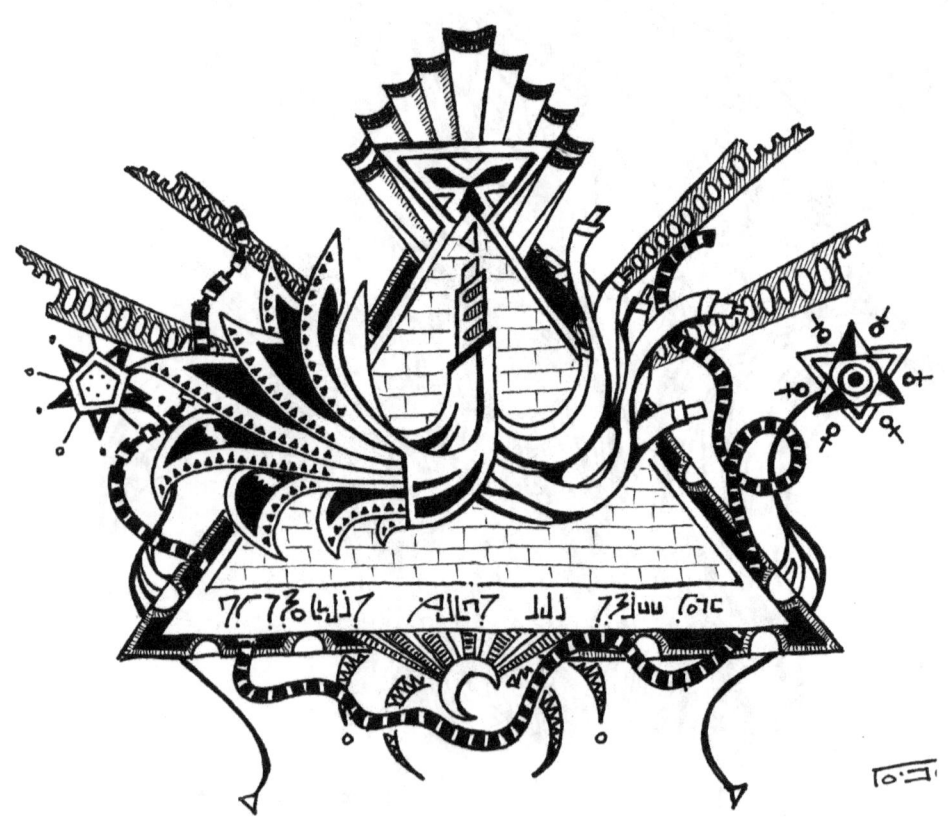

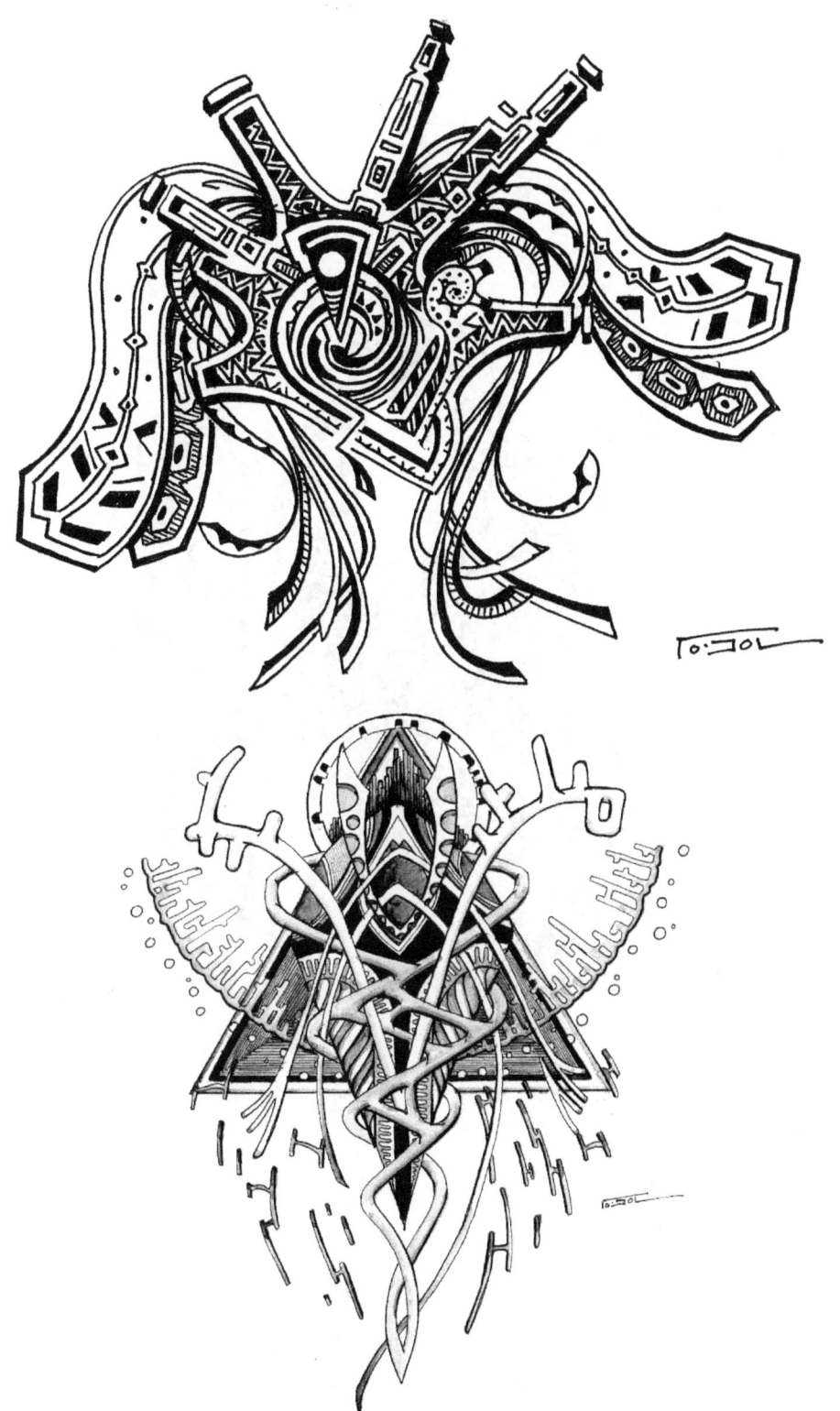

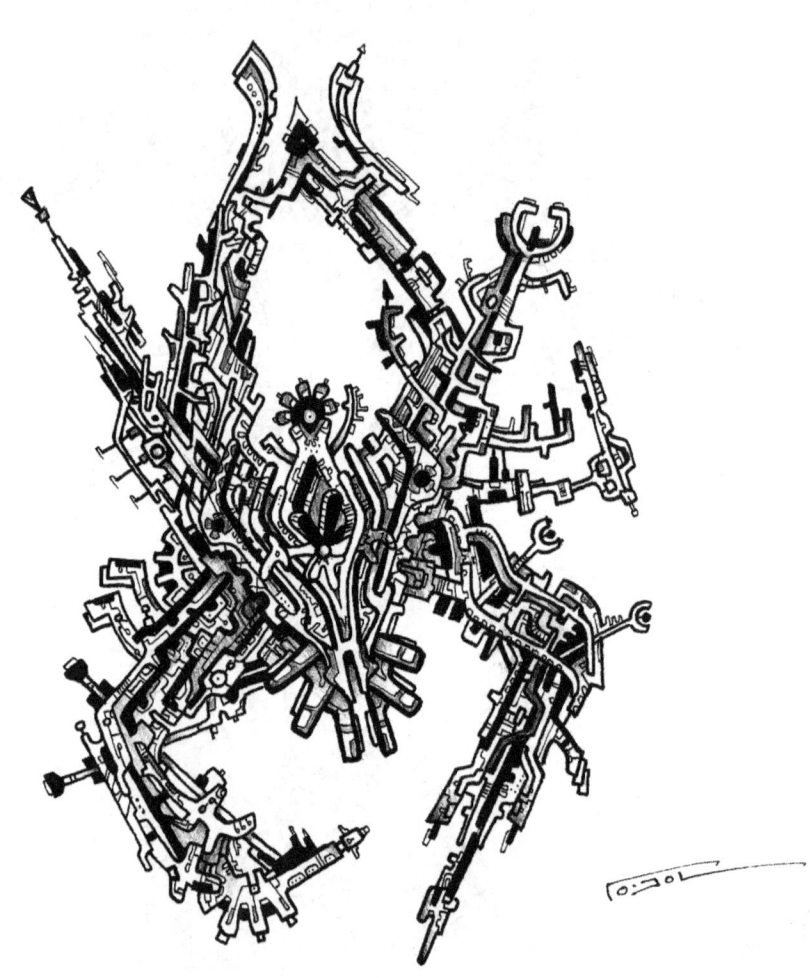

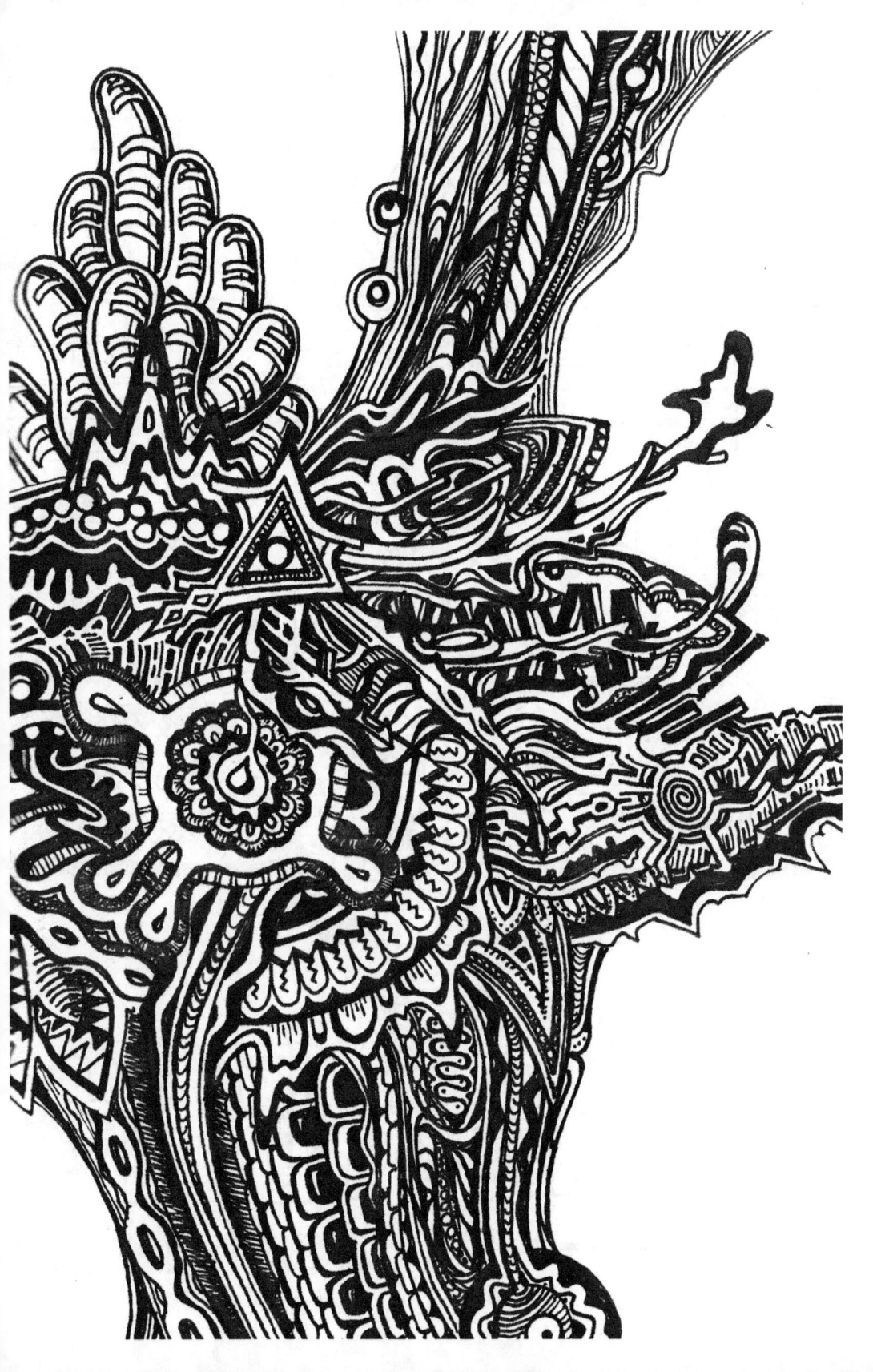

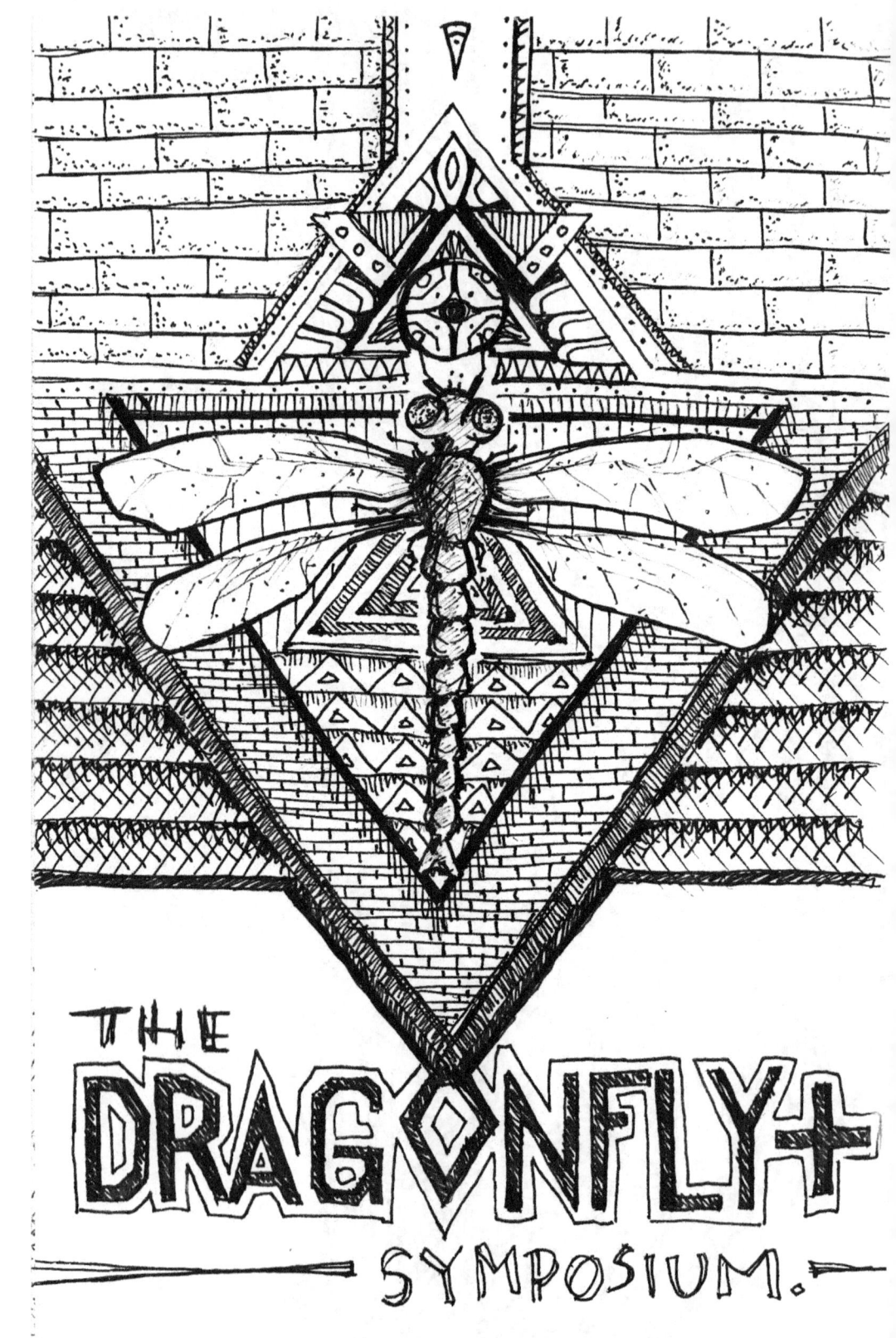

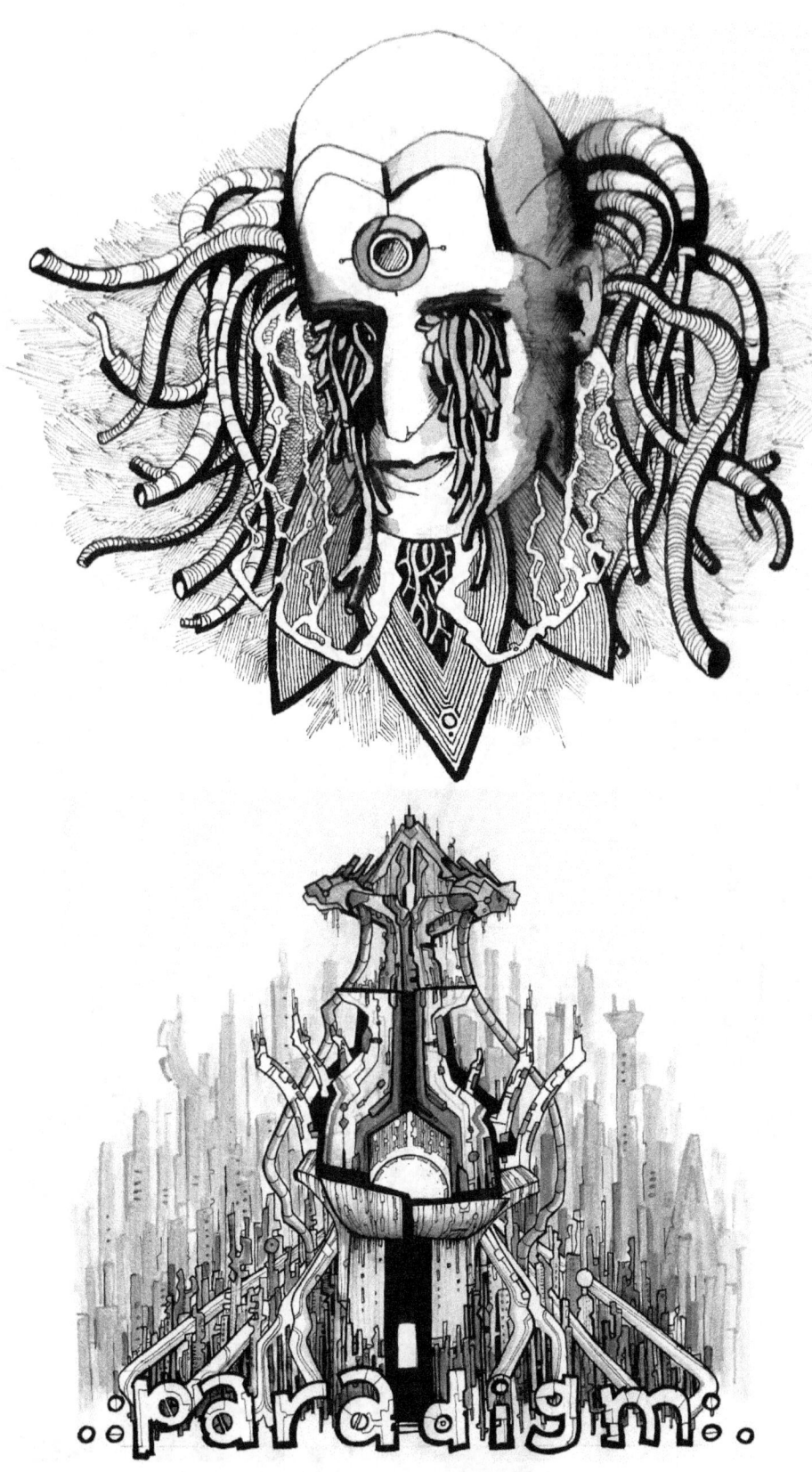

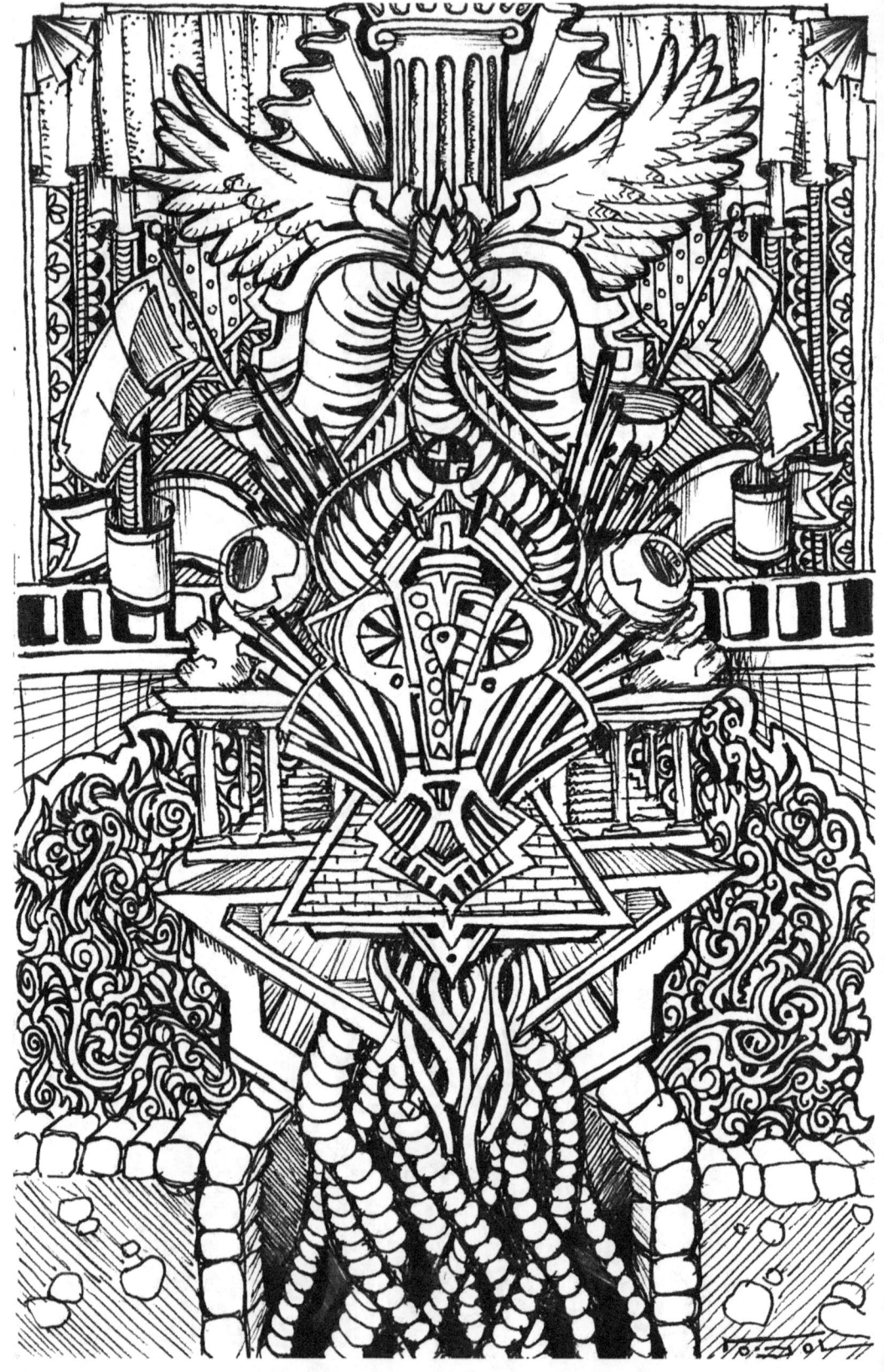

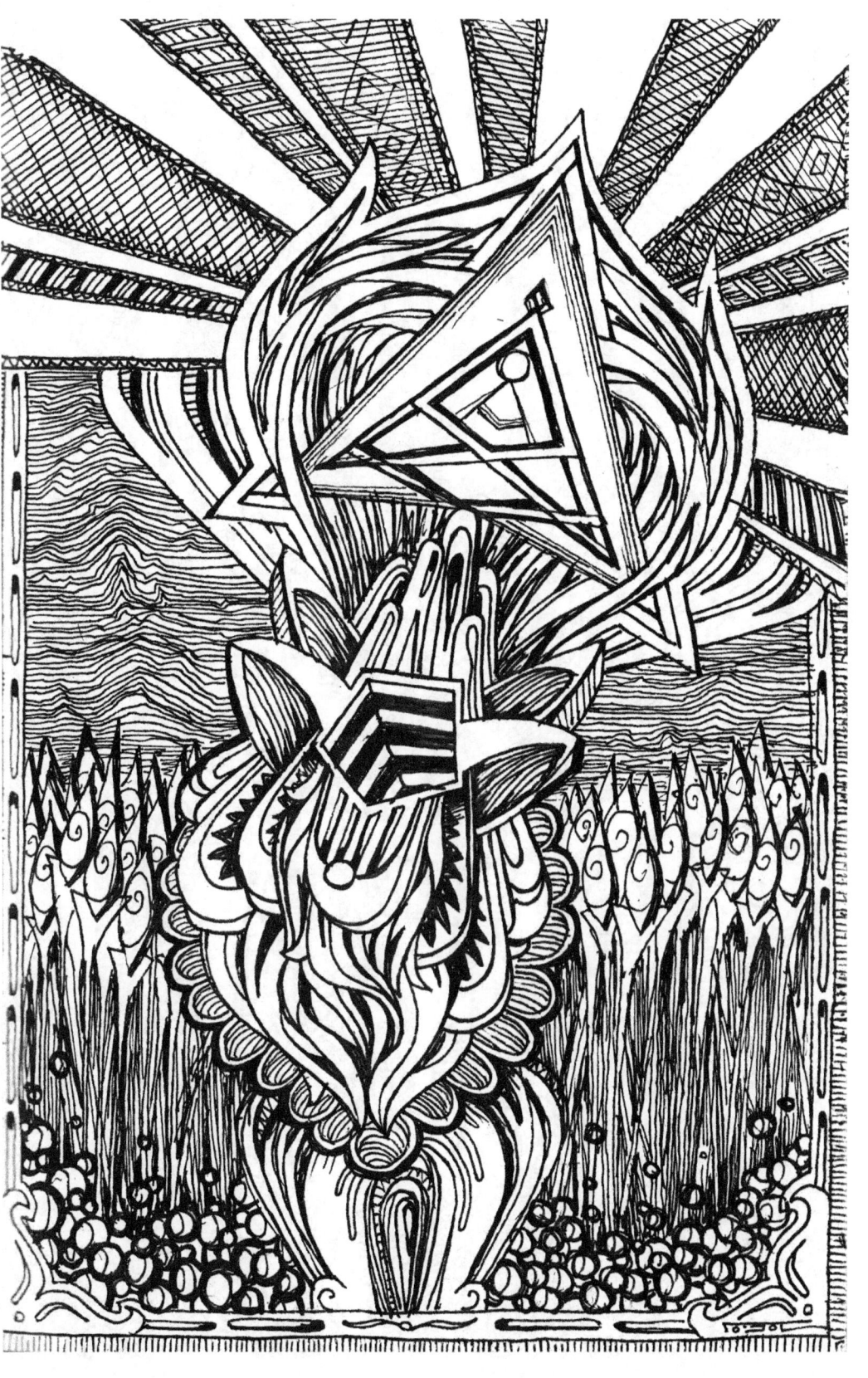

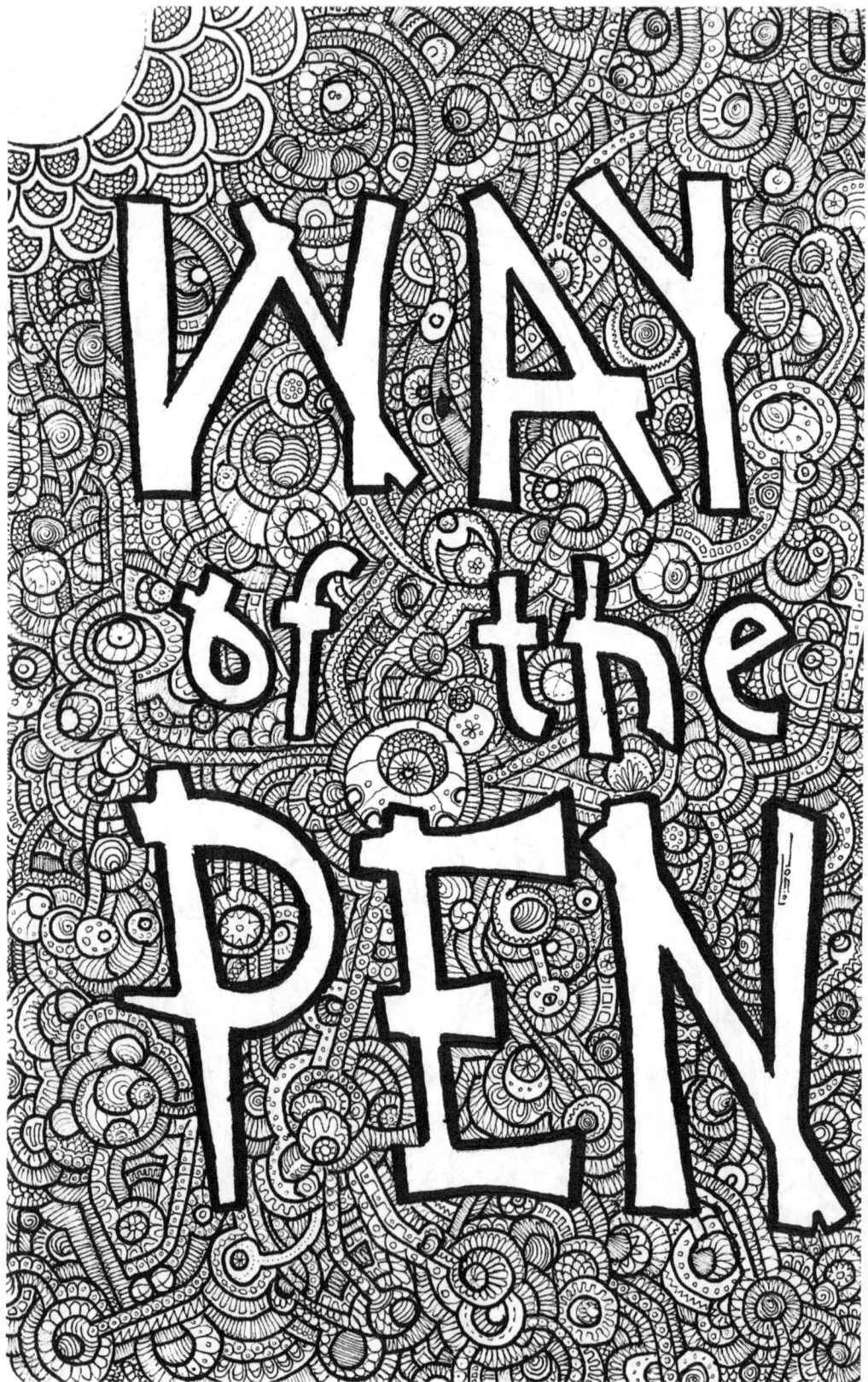

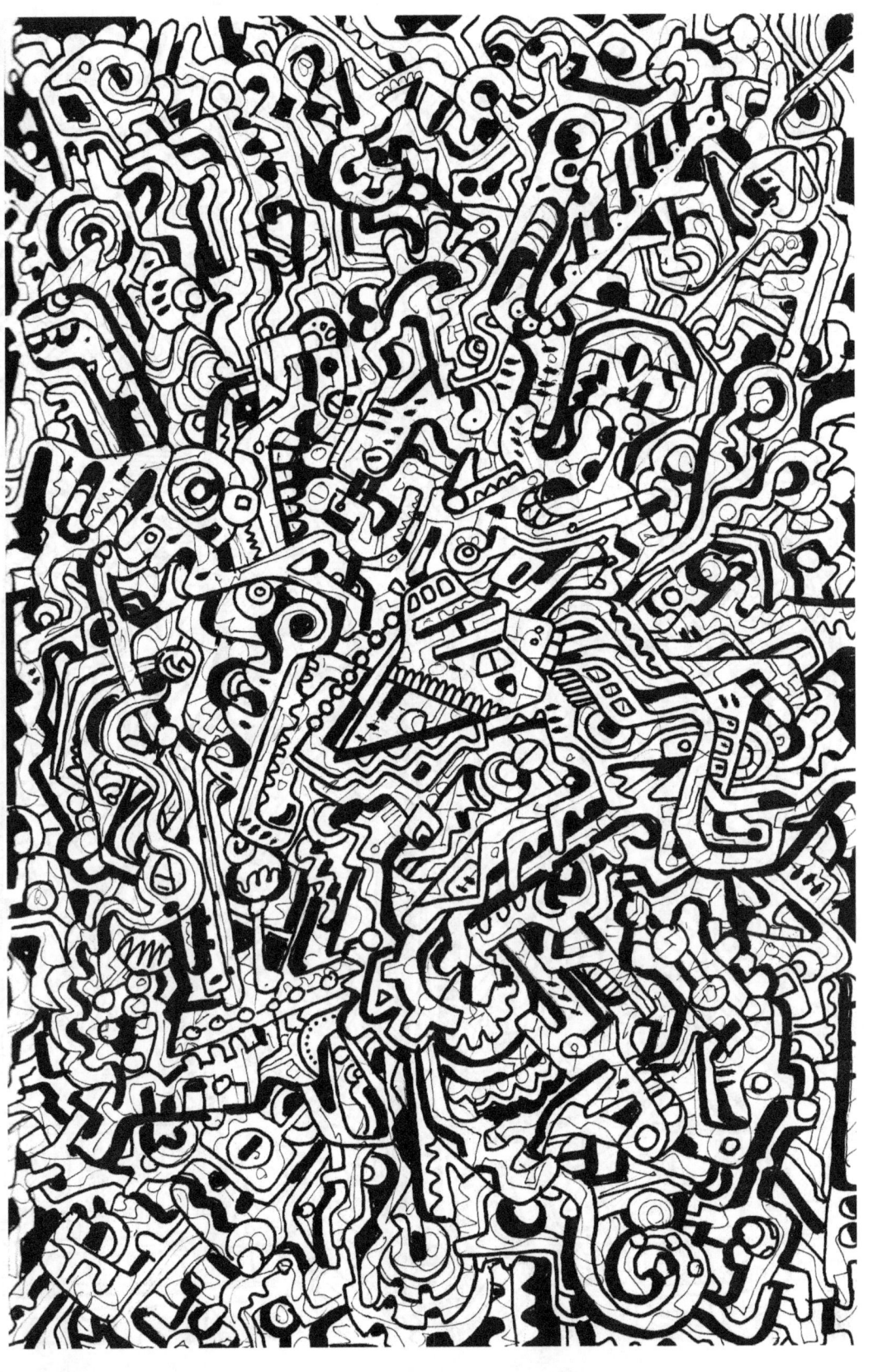

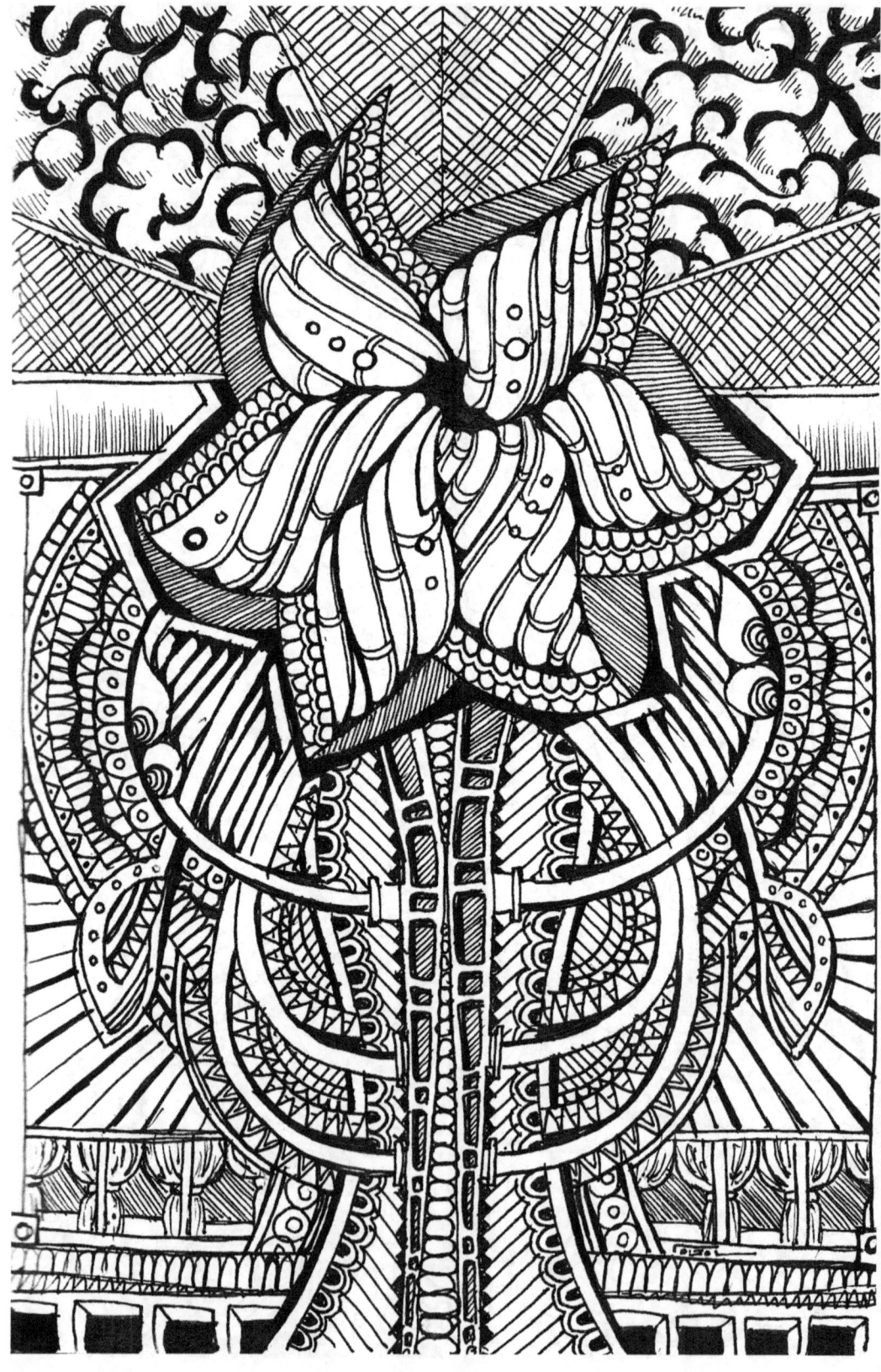

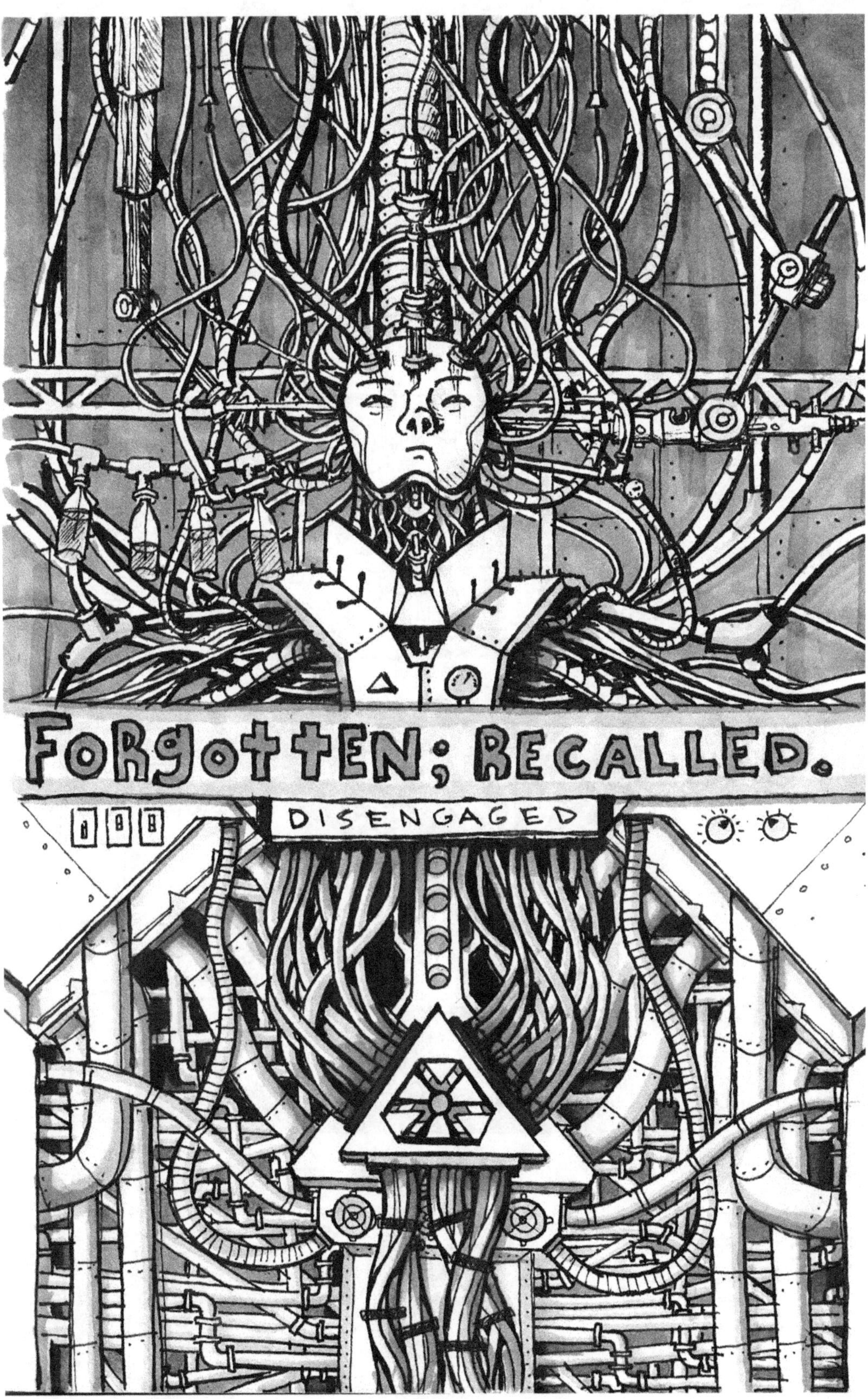

FORGOTTEN; RECALLED.

DISENGAGED

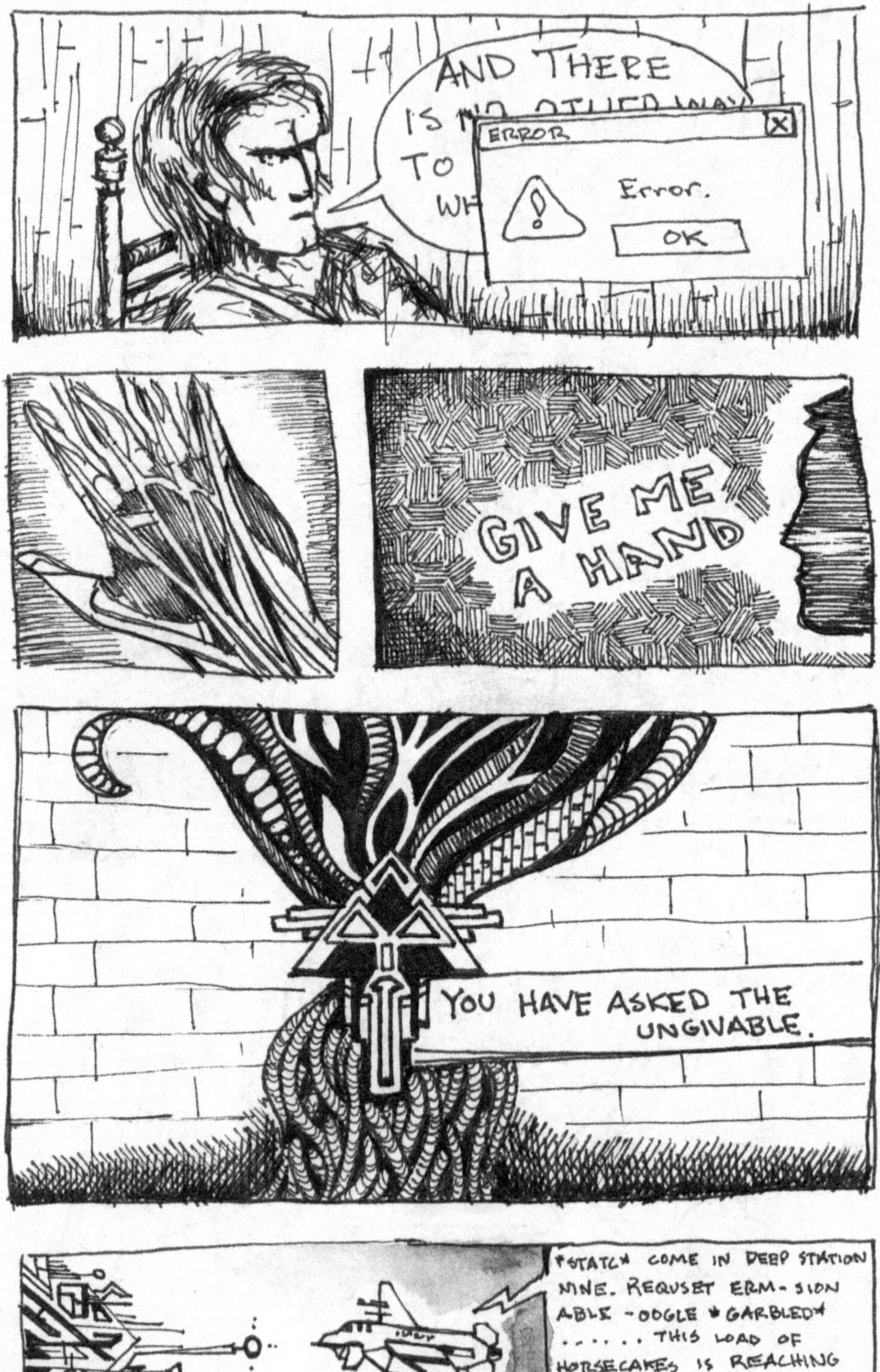

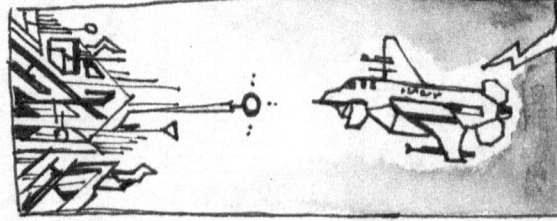

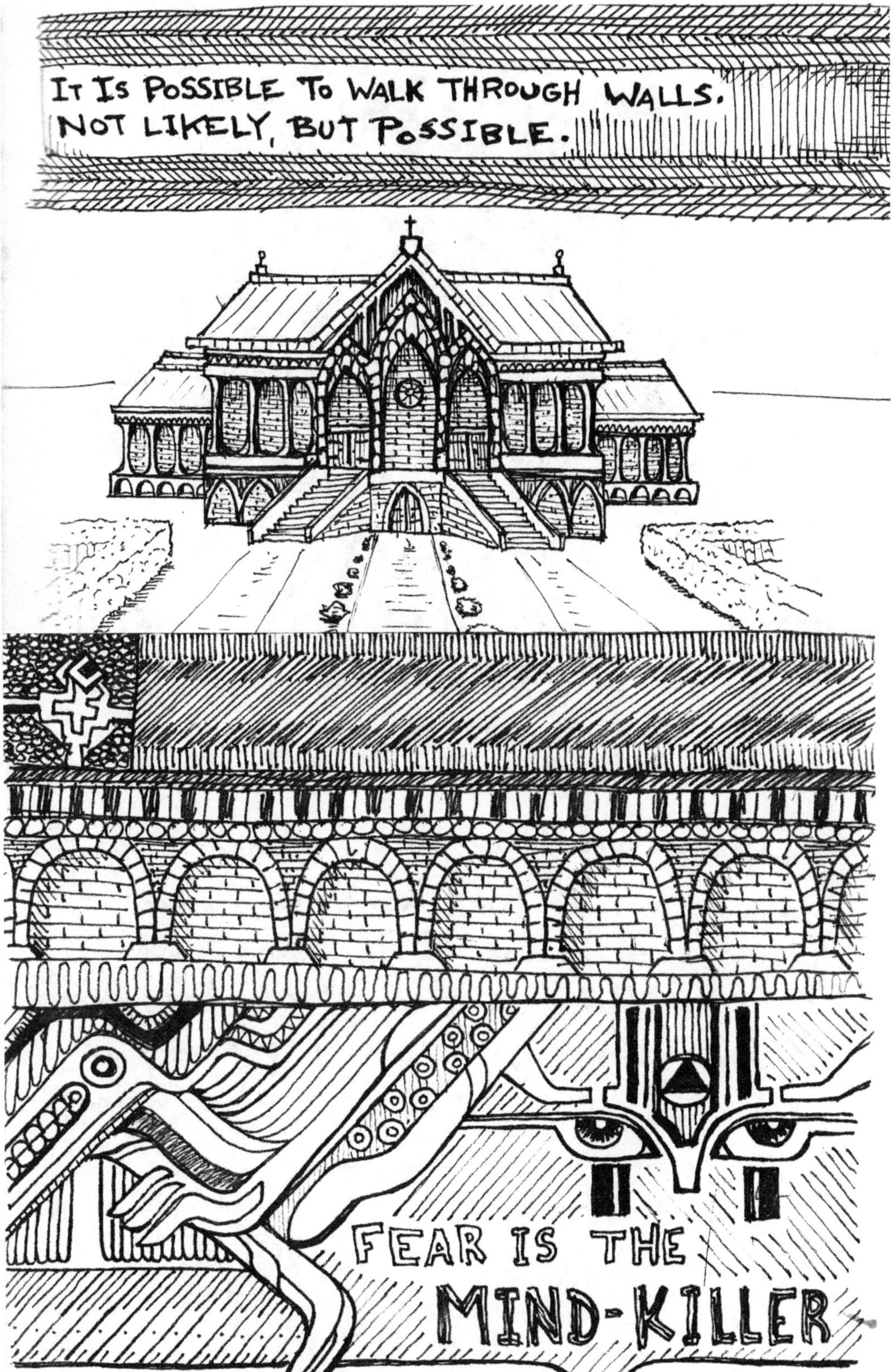

IT IS POSSIBLE TO WALK THROUGH WALLS.
NOT LIKELY, BUT POSSIBLE.
FEAR IS THE
MIND-KILLER

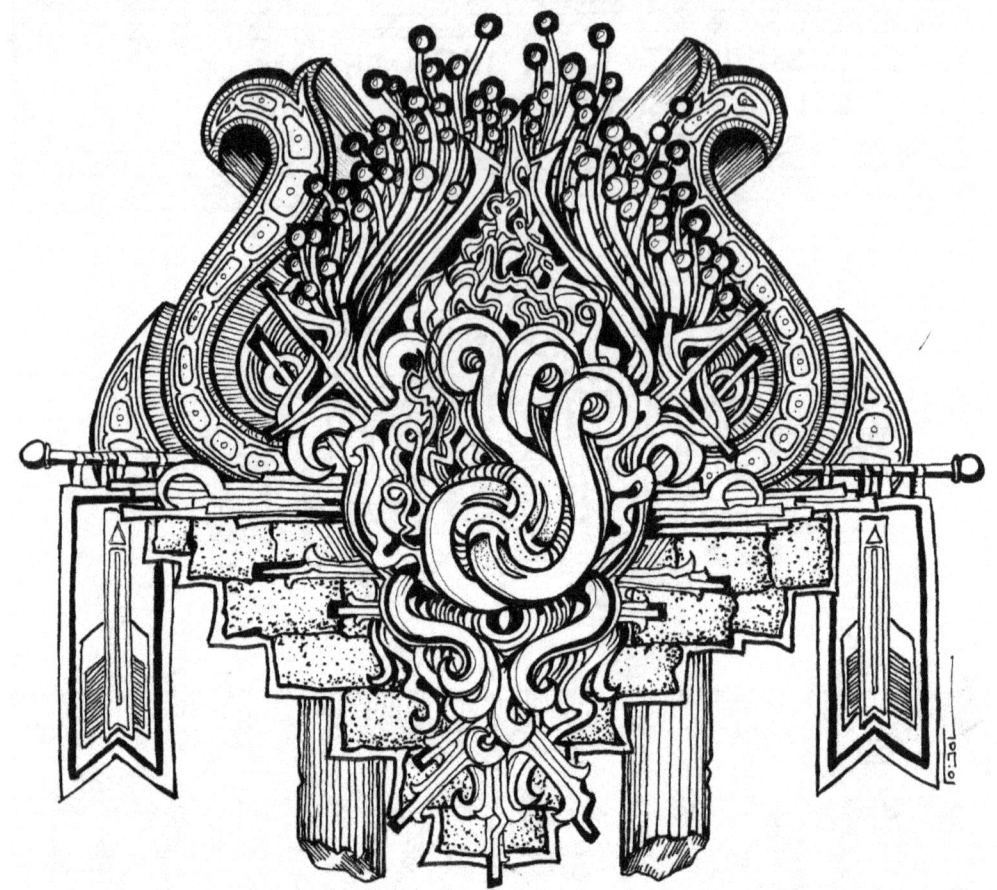

Both nature and the manmade things around us can (and must!) be coaxed into surrendering to us ideas and concepts that can be translated into fulfilling art. Art that is pleasant or interesting to the eyes and challenging or stimulating to the mind.

WE MUST CREATE.

(HUMANS)

Why do we enjoy creating things? Why do we have this urge? Is it a selfish thing, to be able to claim some accomplishment, to claim a creative ability and to be able to claim something other people like as your own? Or is it simply a quest for beauty? A quest for something previously unseen? To create some proof that we existed at some point in time and space? Or is it purely cathartic in nature? Something else? All of these?

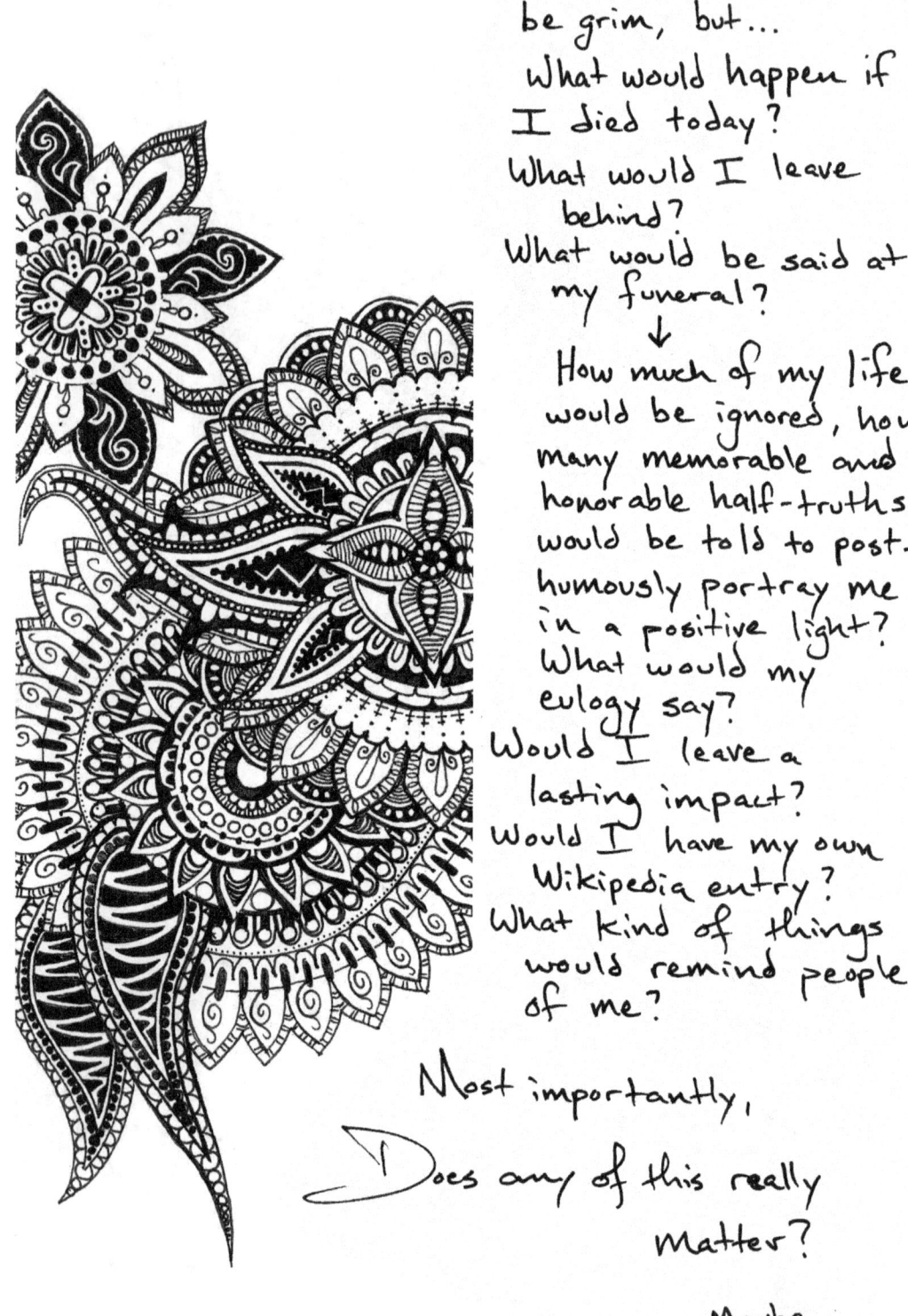

I don't mean to
be grim, but...
What would happen if
I died today?
What would I leave
    behind?
What would be said at
    my funeral?
        ↓
    How much of my life
    would be ignored, how
many memorable and
honorable half-truths
would be told to post-
humously portray me
in a positive light?
What would my
eulogy say?
Would I leave a
    lasting impact?
Would I have my own
    Wikipedia entry?
What kind of things
    would remind people
    of me?

Most importantly,

Does any of this really
            Matter?

            Maybe.

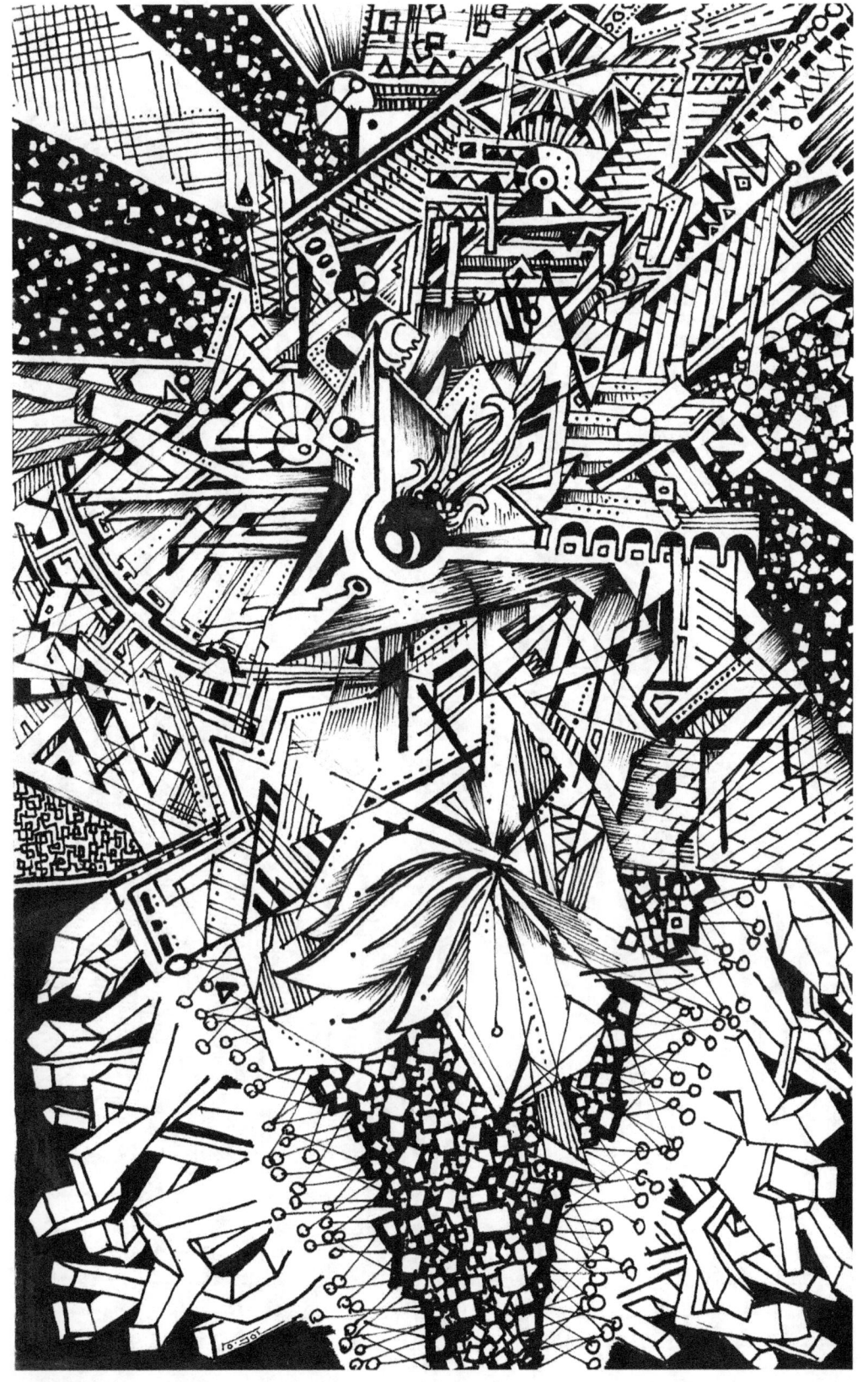

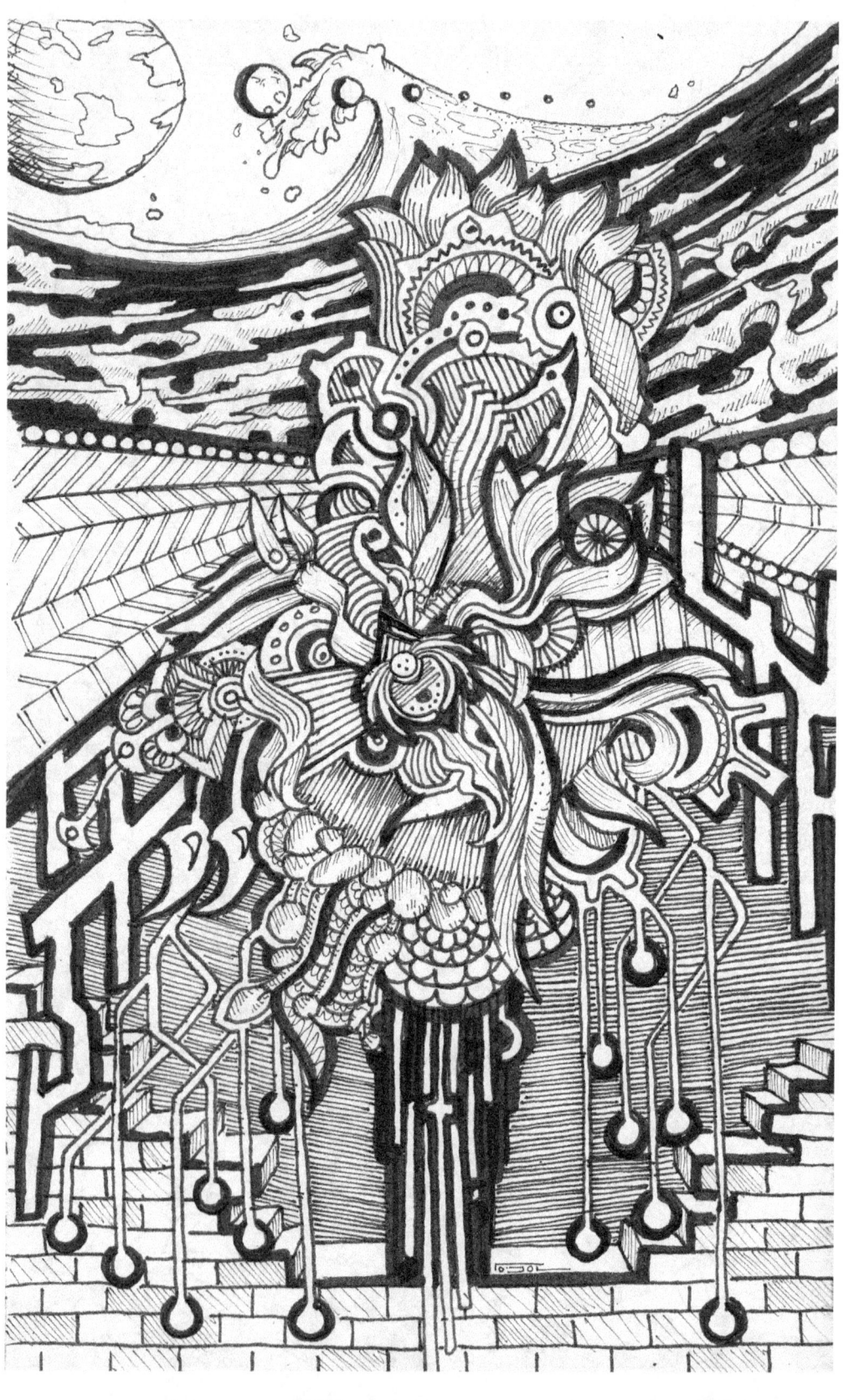

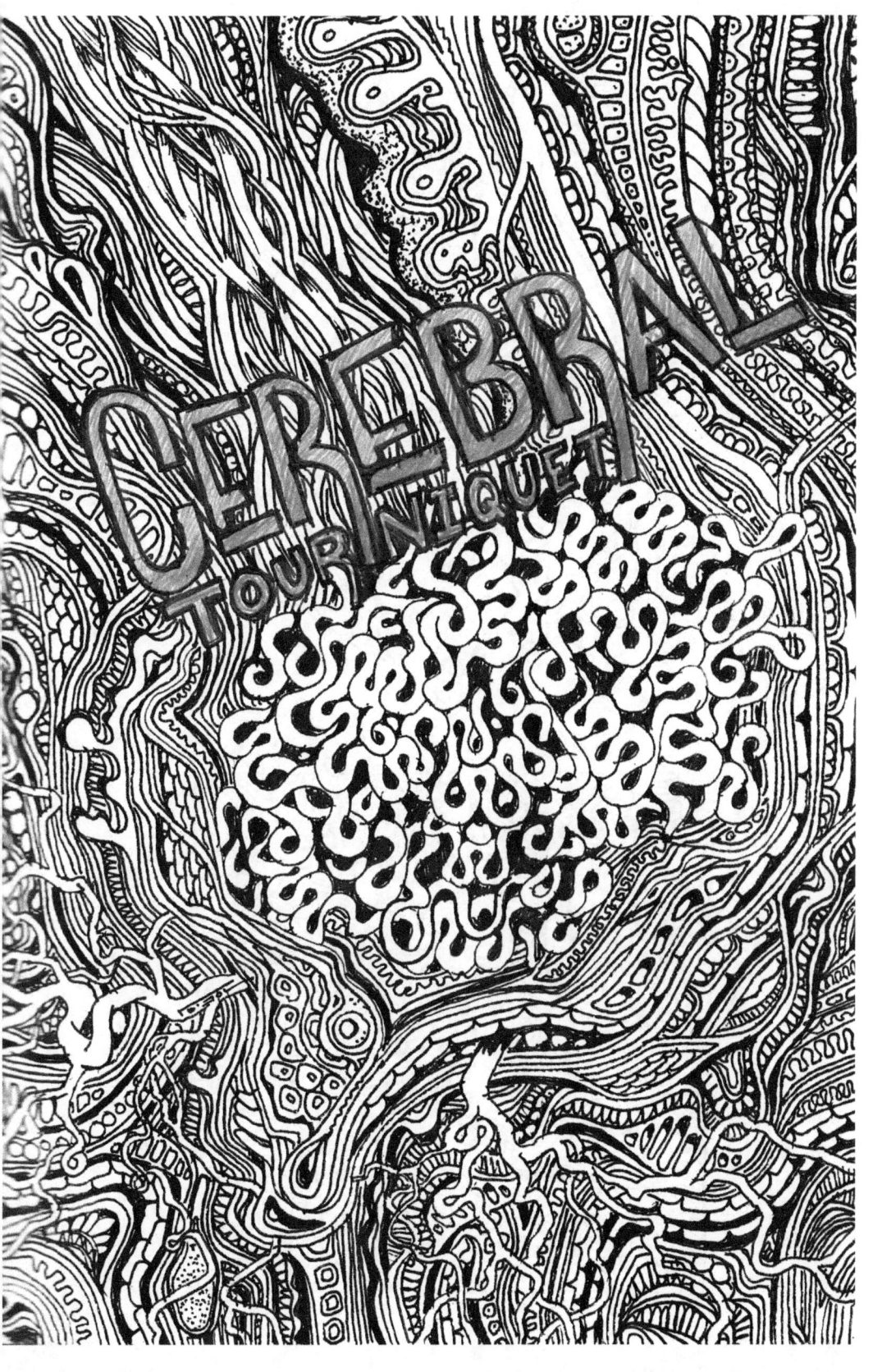

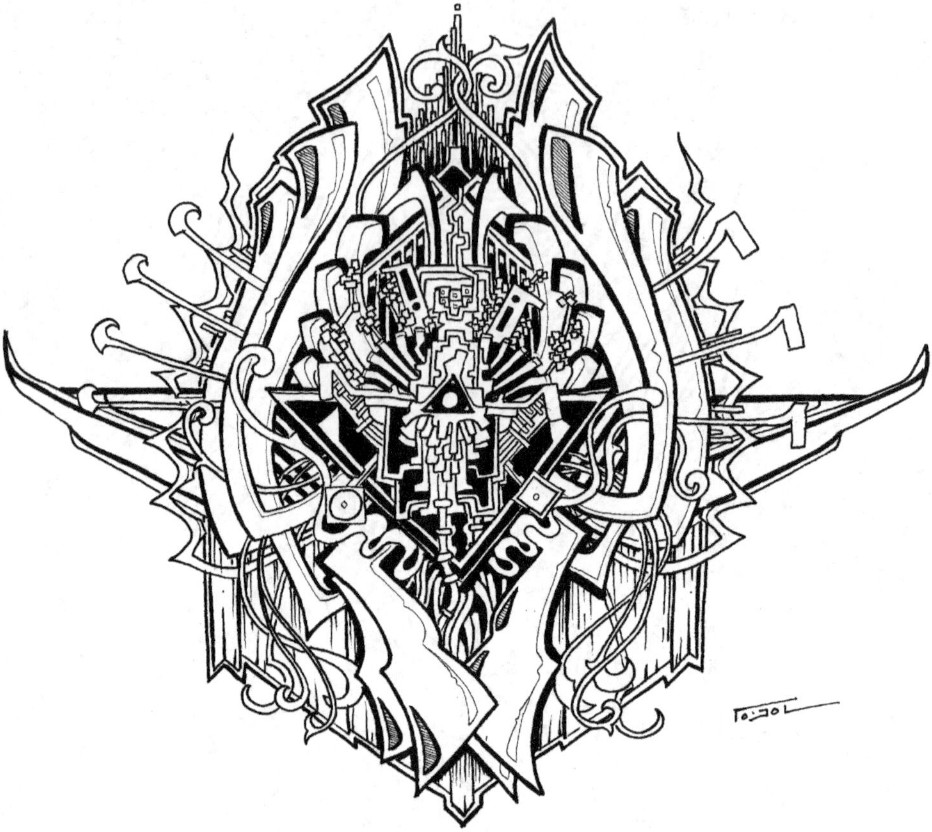

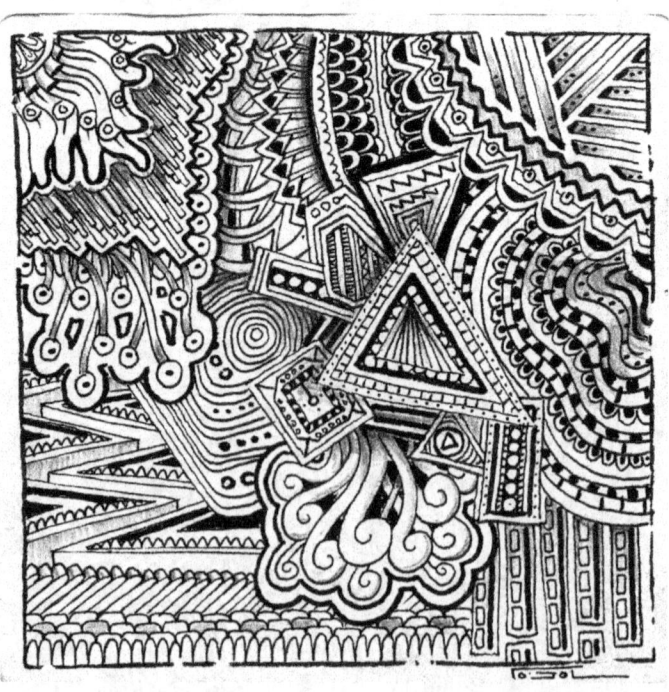

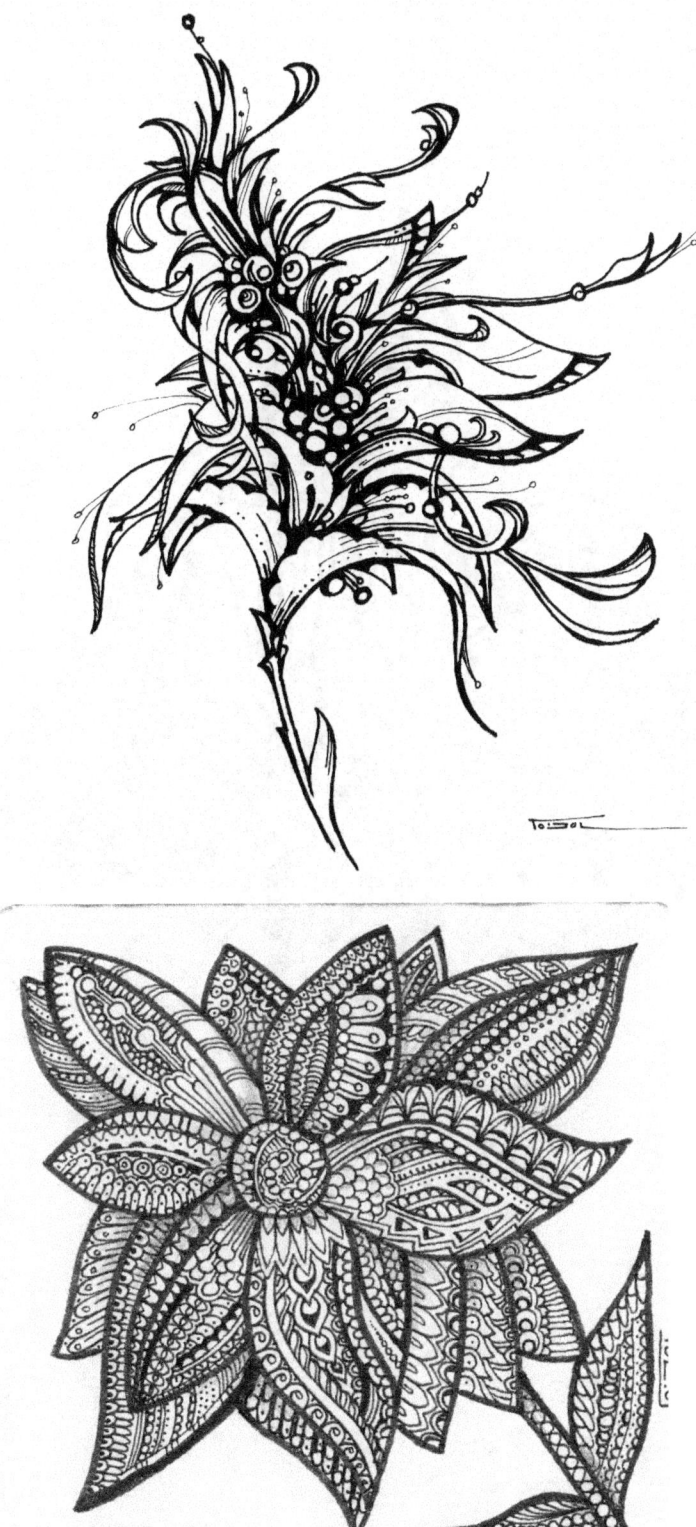

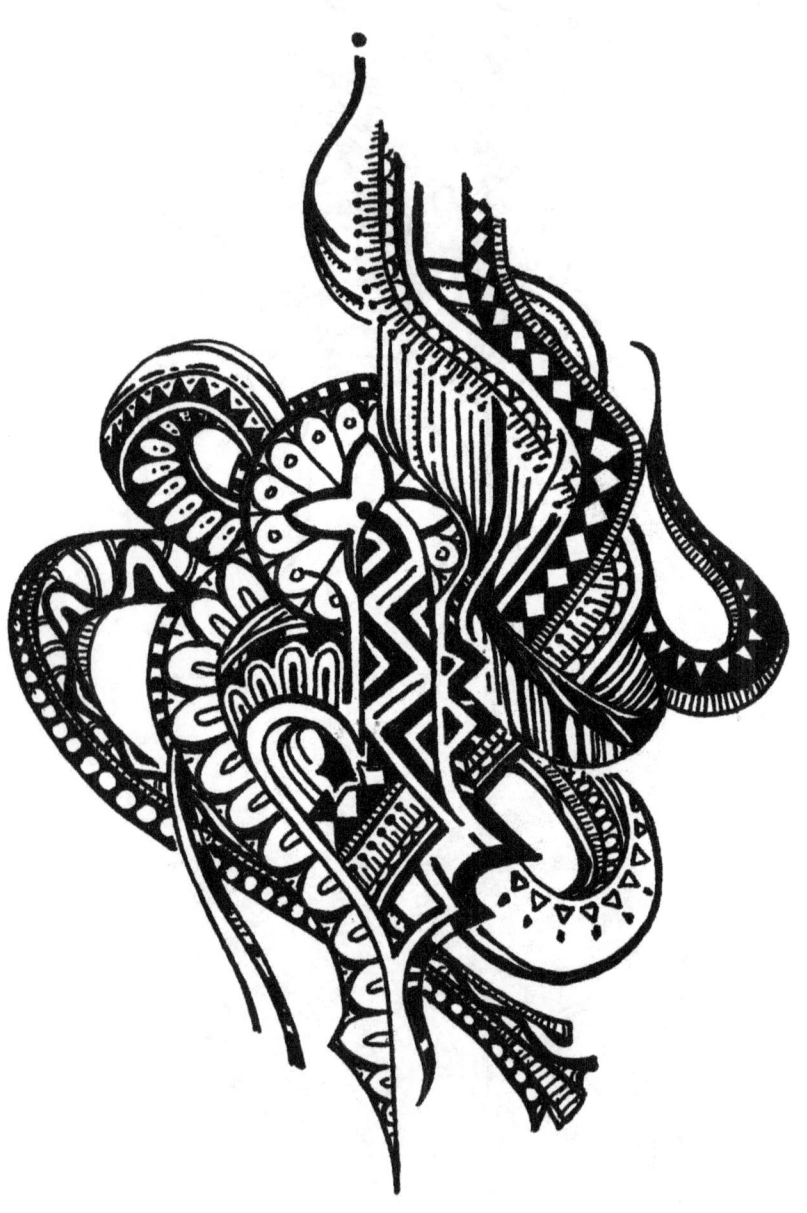

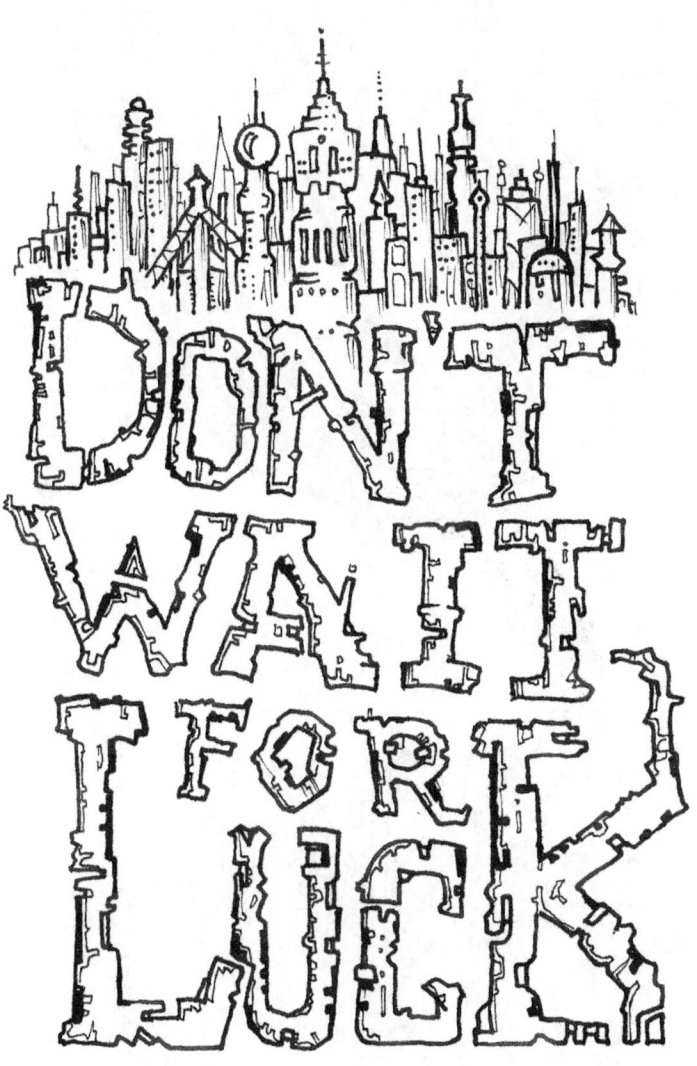

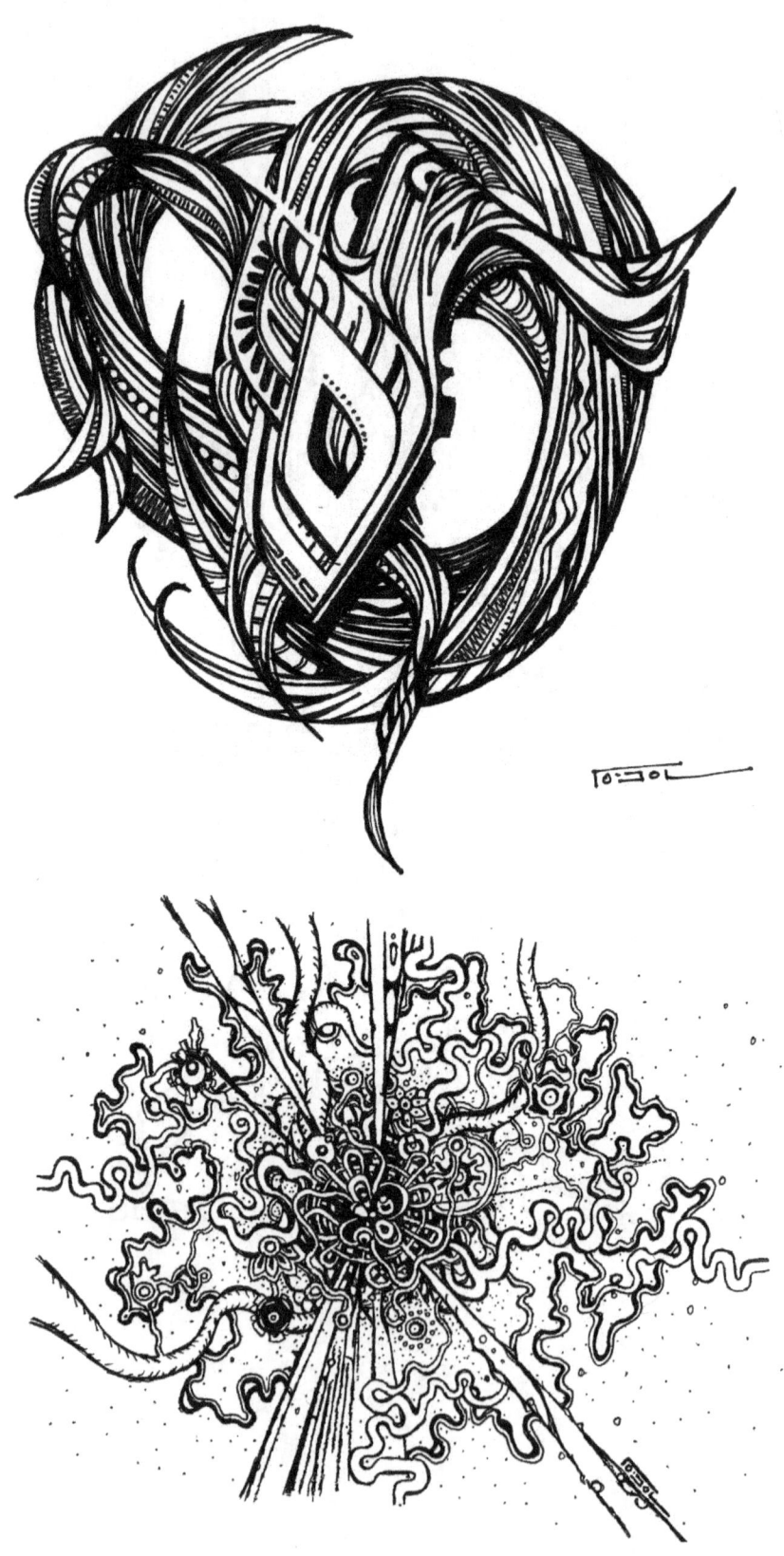

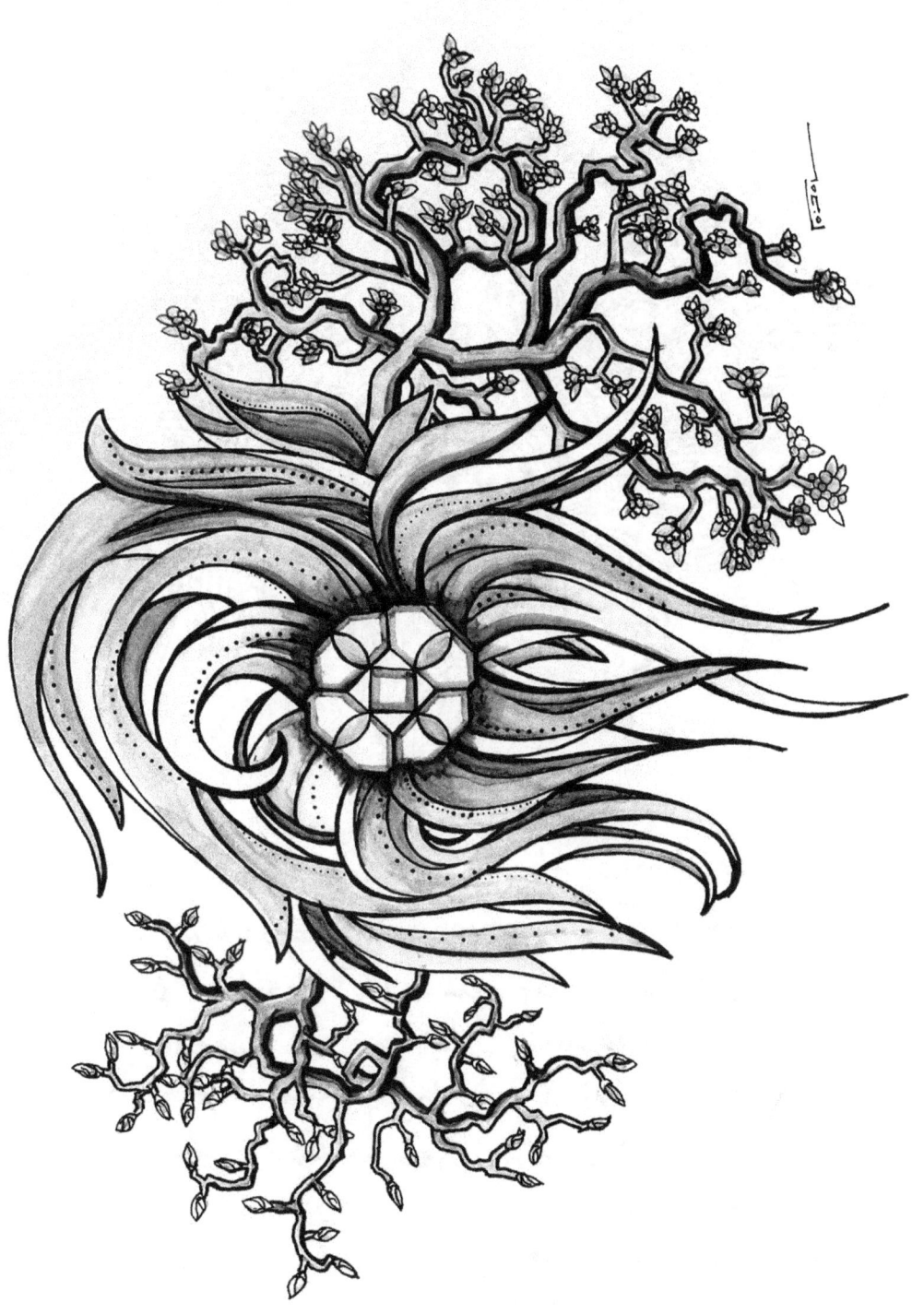

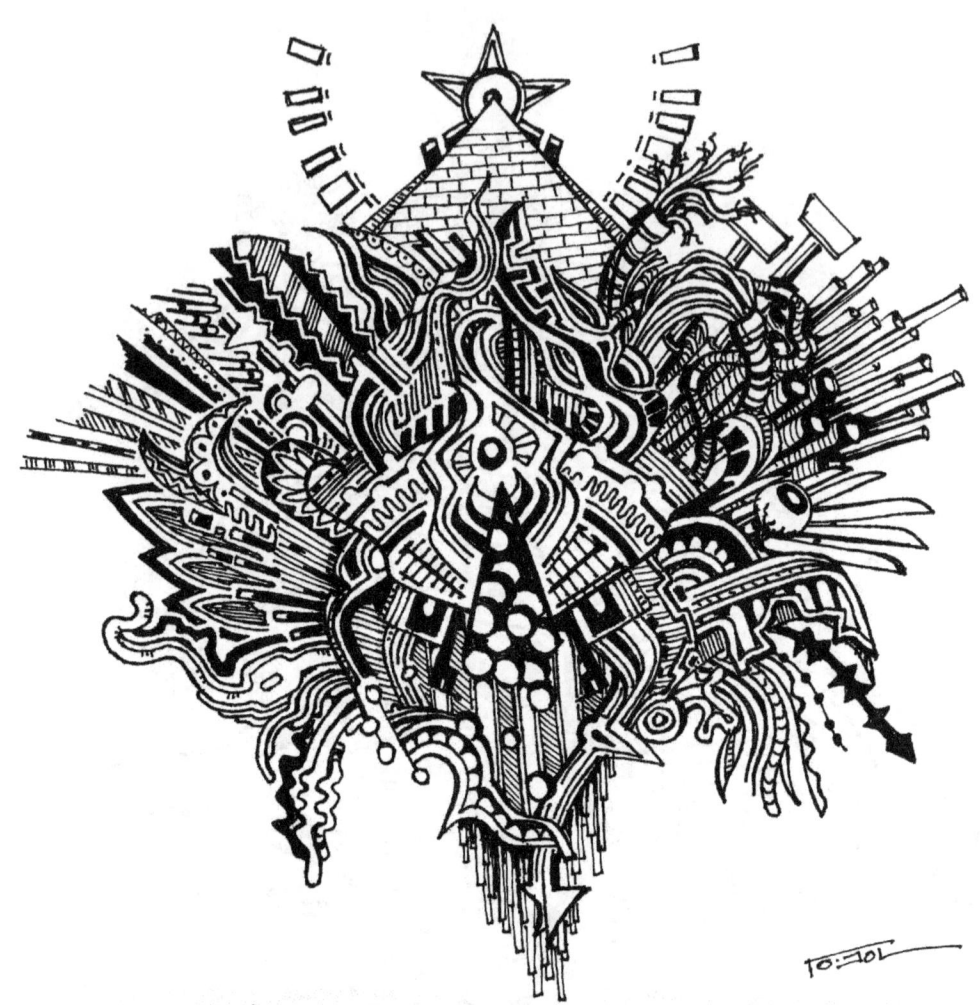

Everything that is beautiful (or
has some other redeeming quality) is
beautiful in itself and by itself. A thing
does not become better or worse
because of how much praise it receives.
Something beautiful, something truly
alluring, needs nothing. Is a beautiful
diamond made less, or worse, simply
because it is not praised?

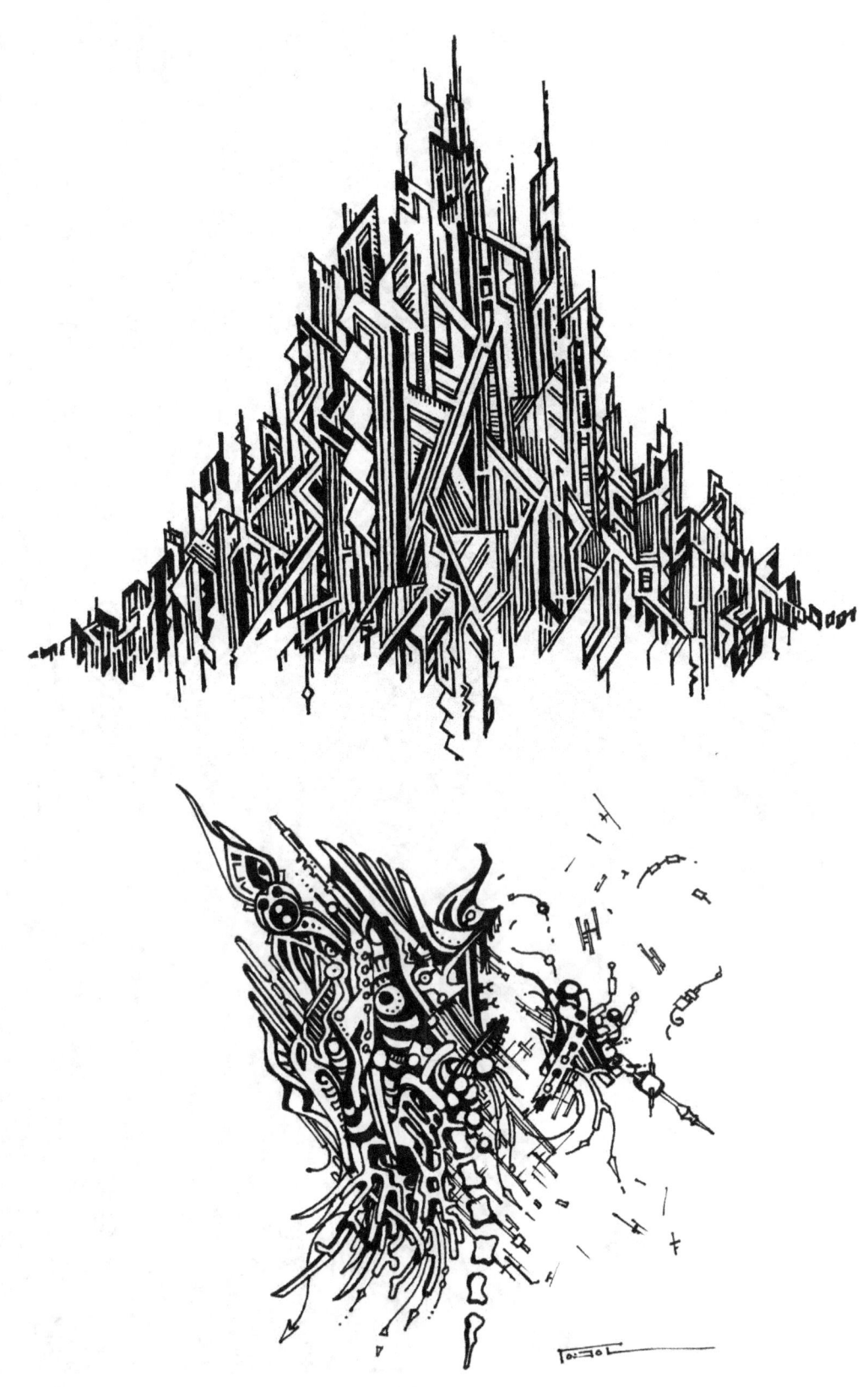

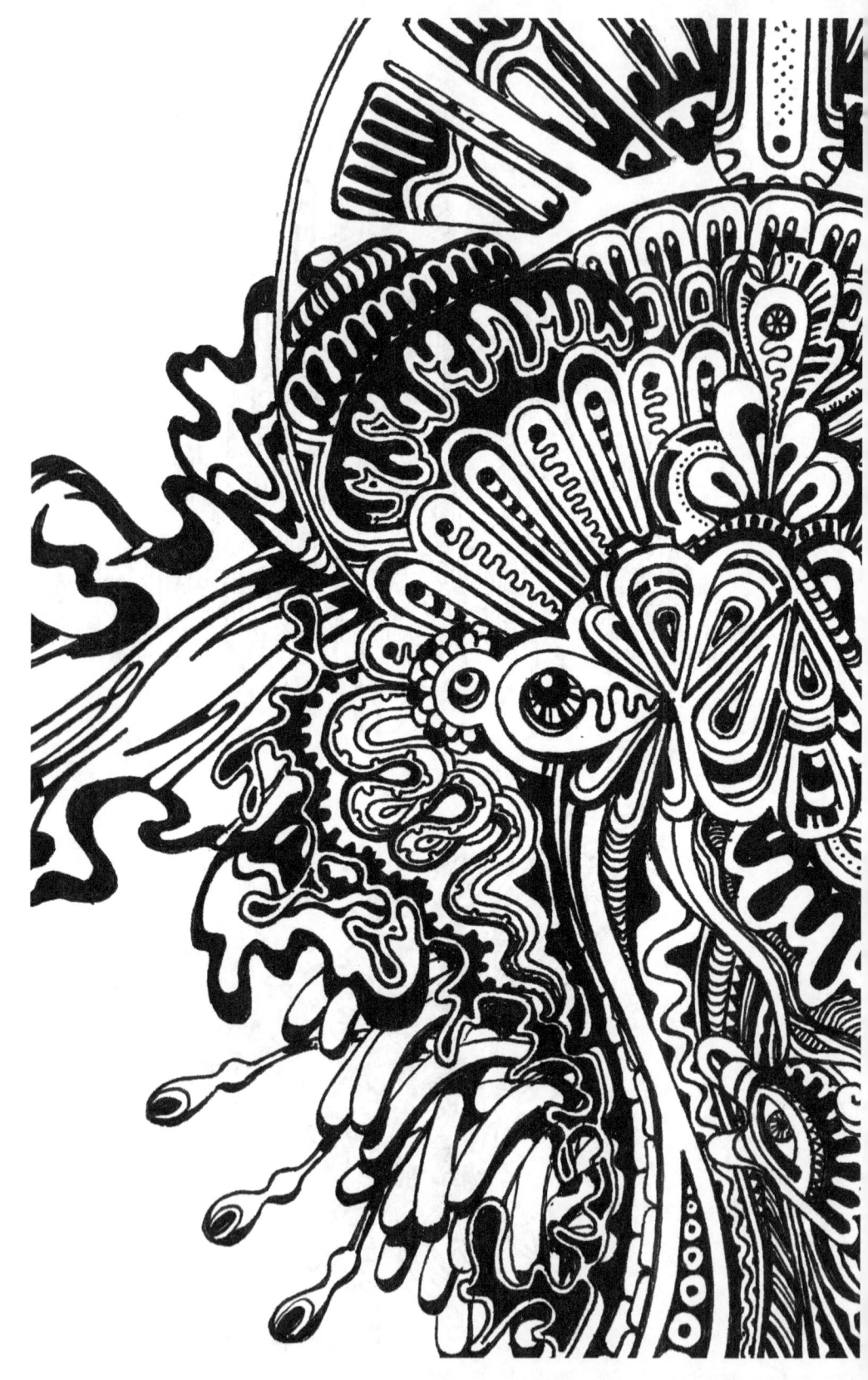

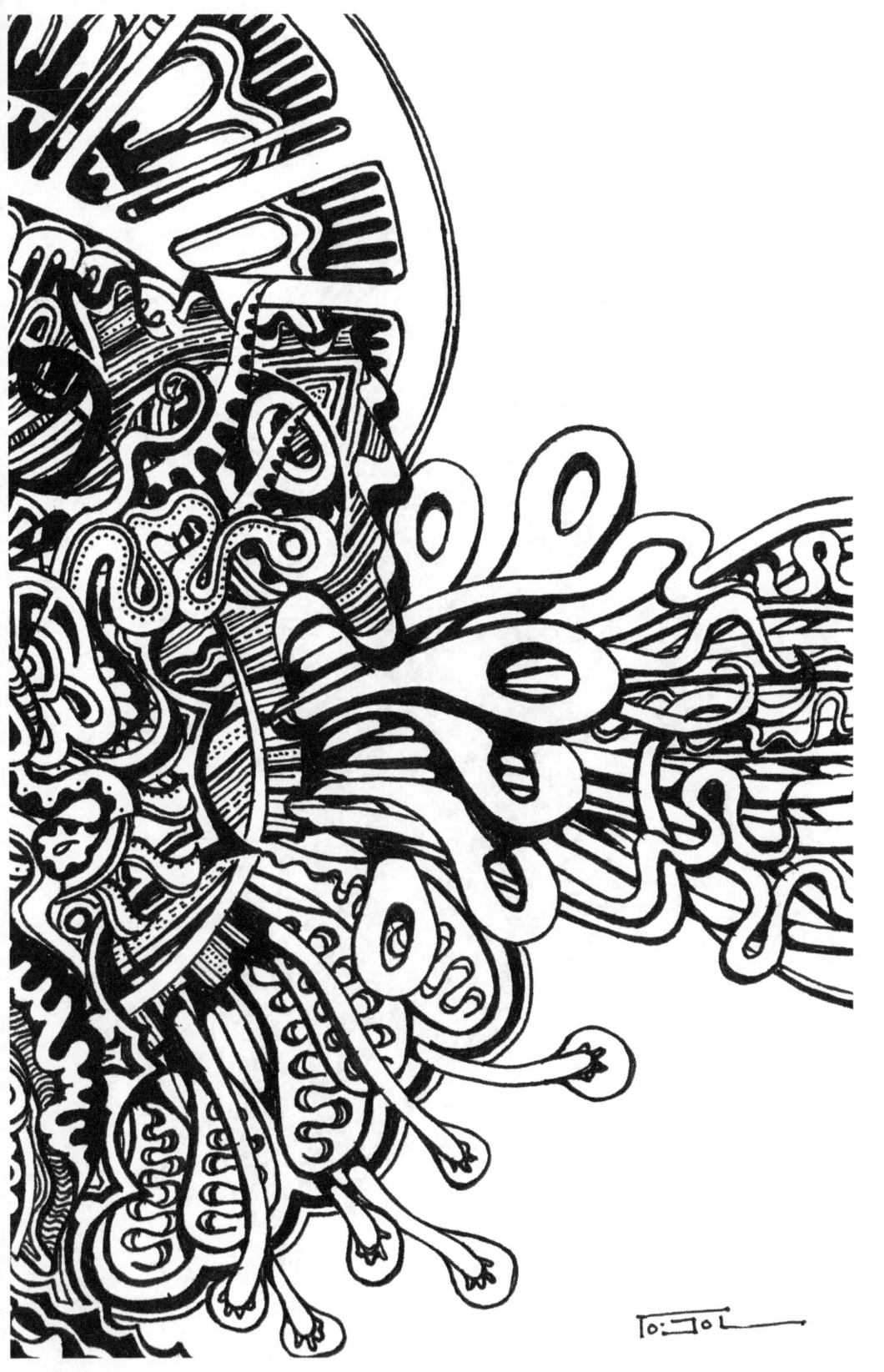

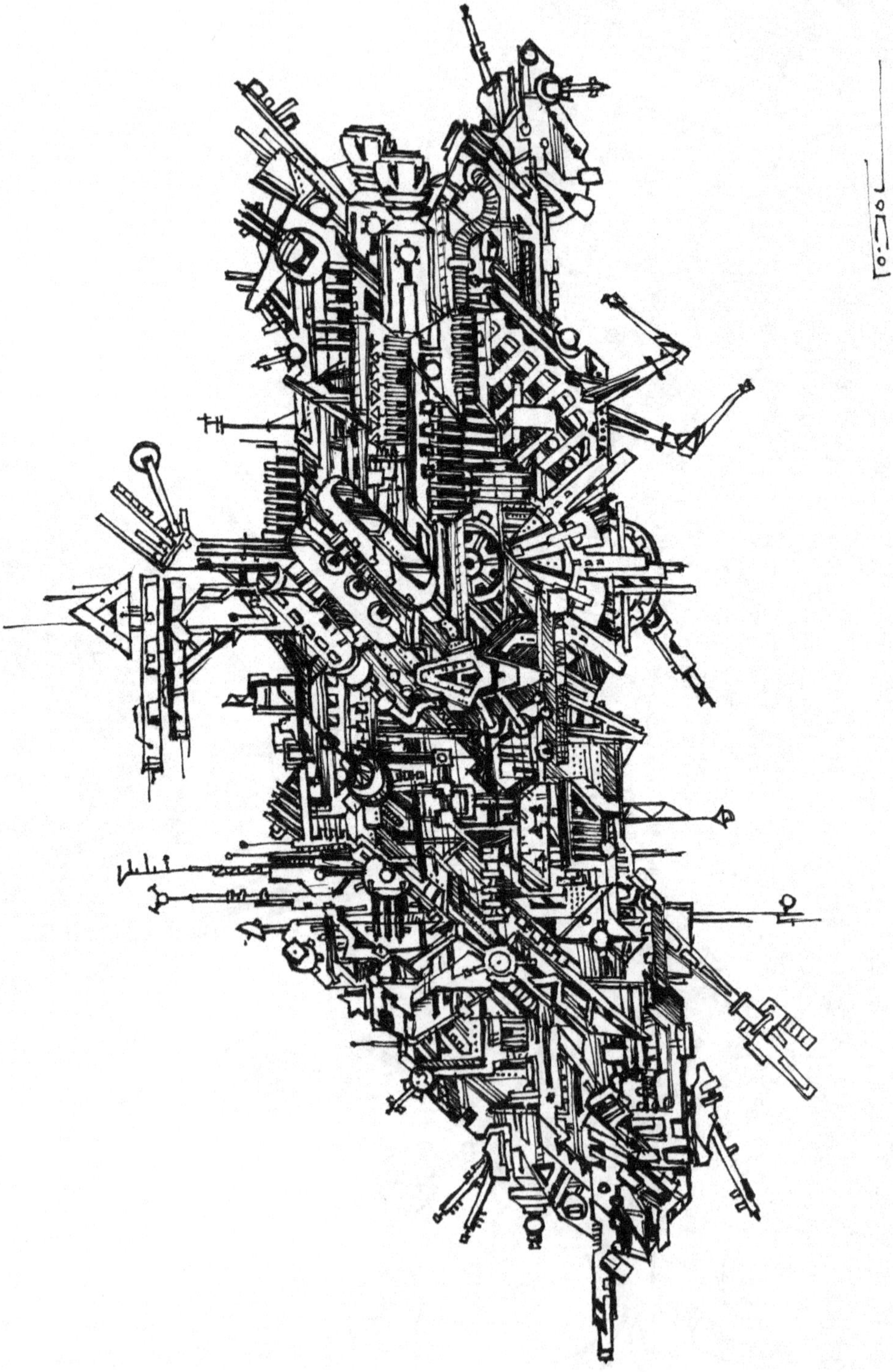

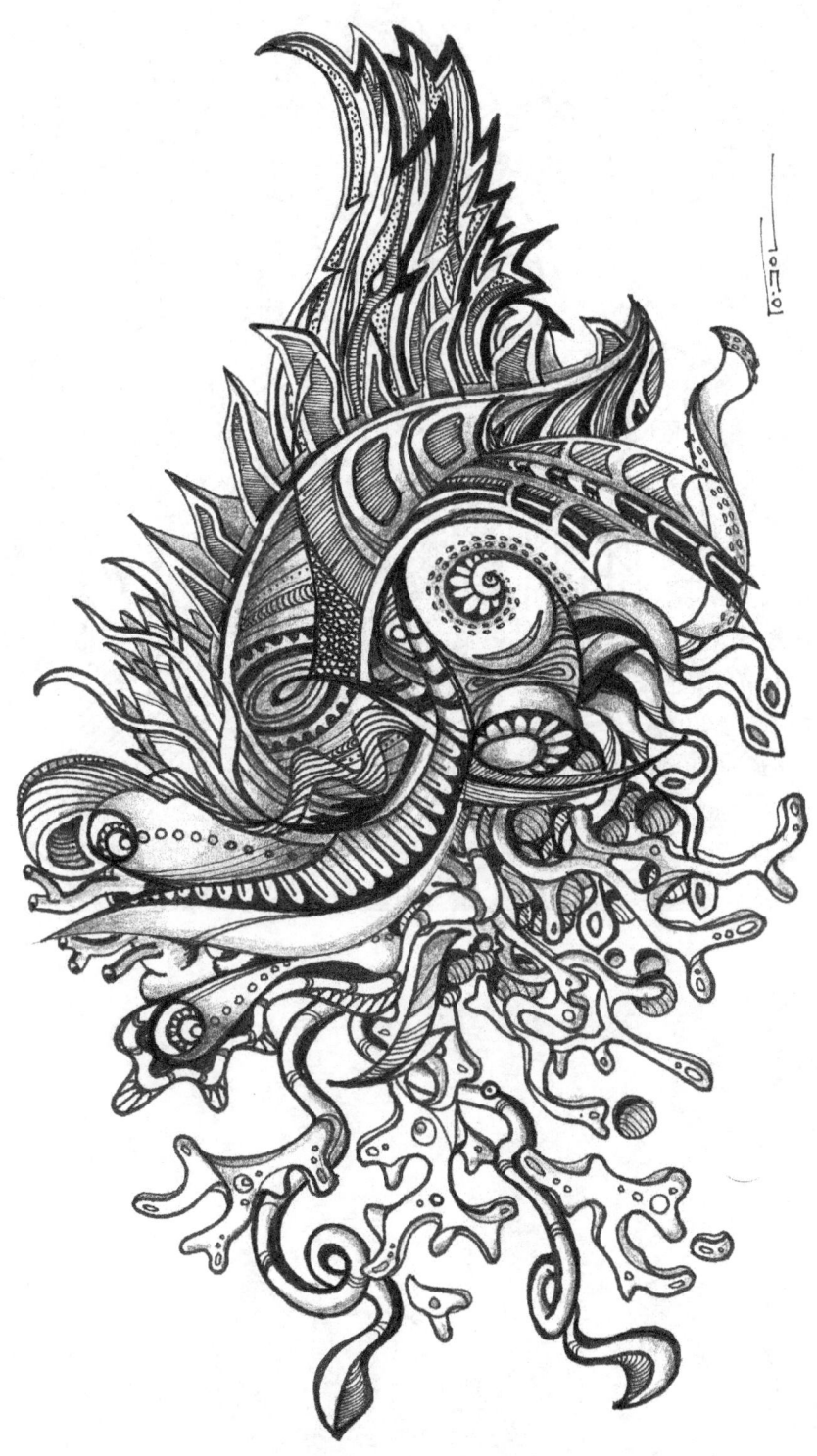

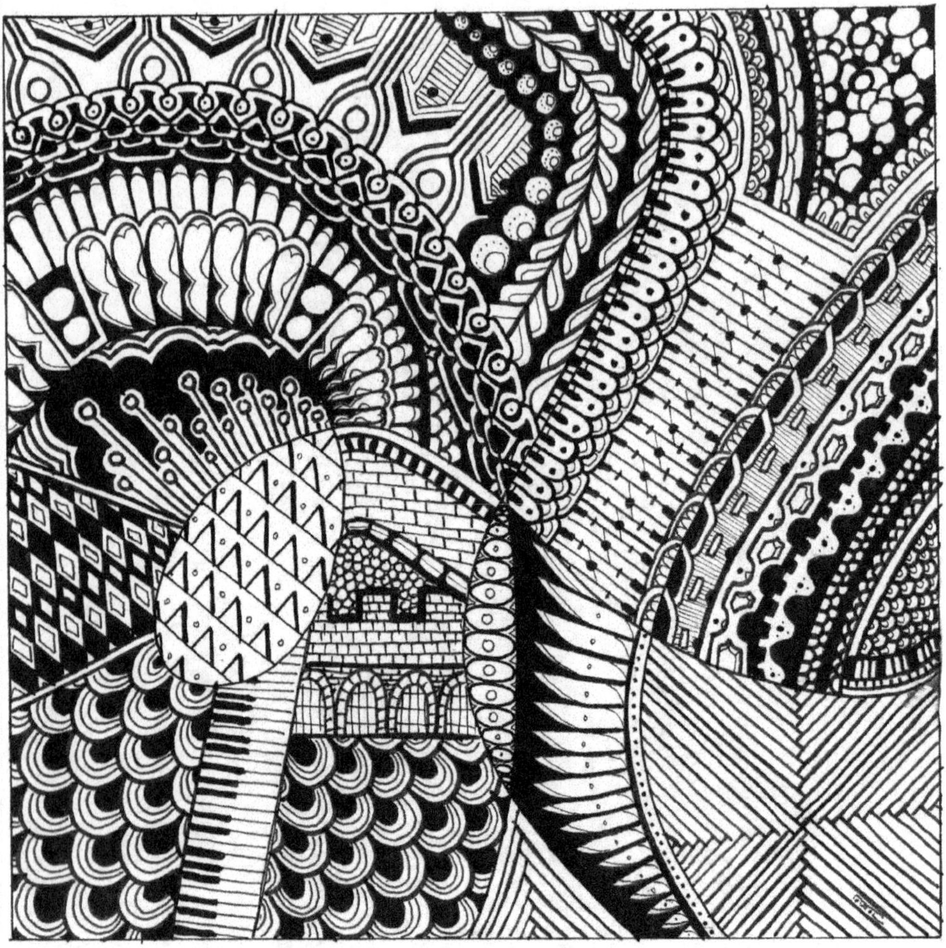

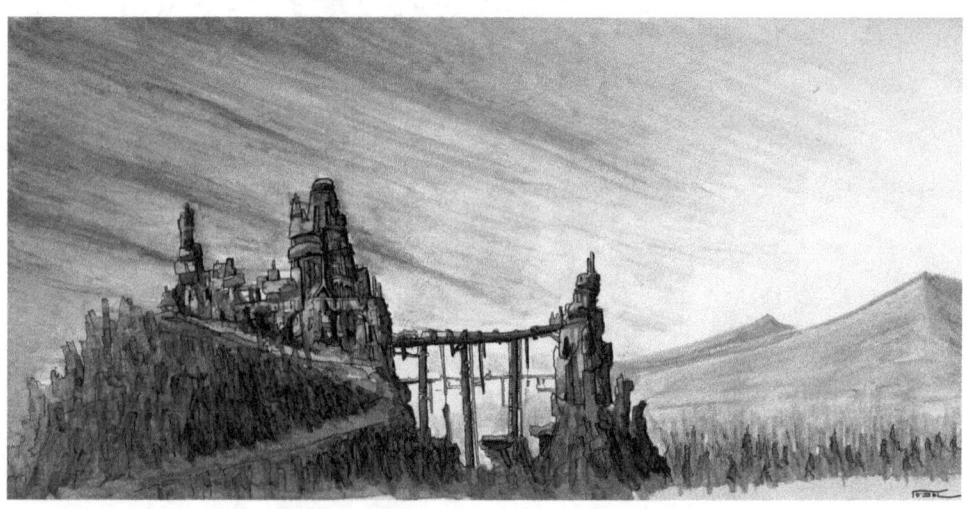

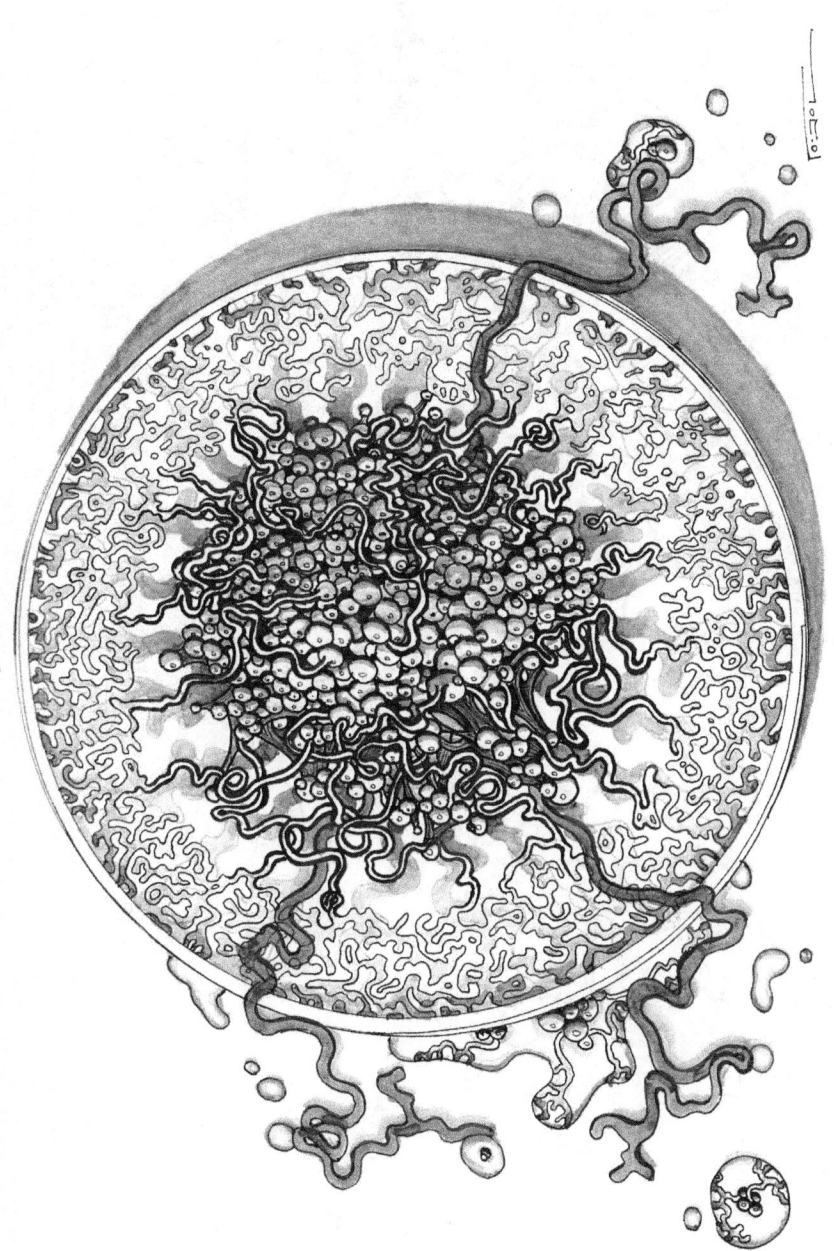

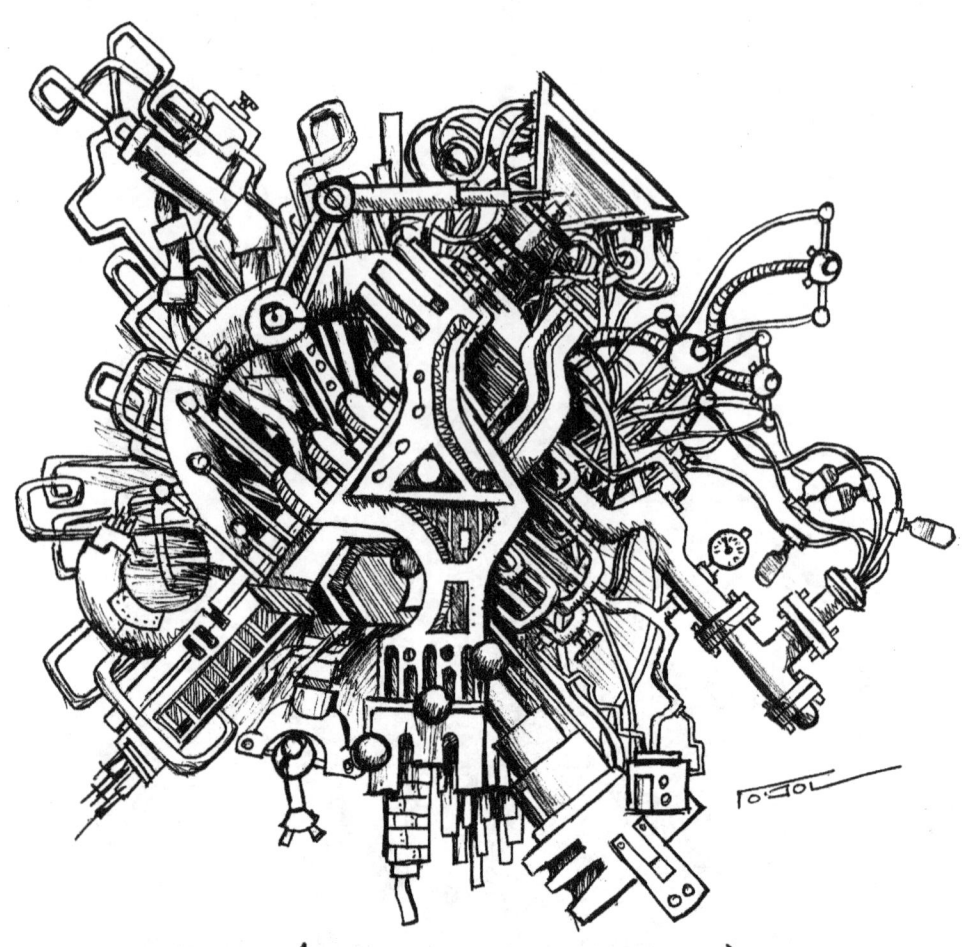

Find something you really enjoy
    doing, and then do that as
much as possible. Make time
for the things you love.
   → "Lost time is
        never found again."

          —Ben Franklin.

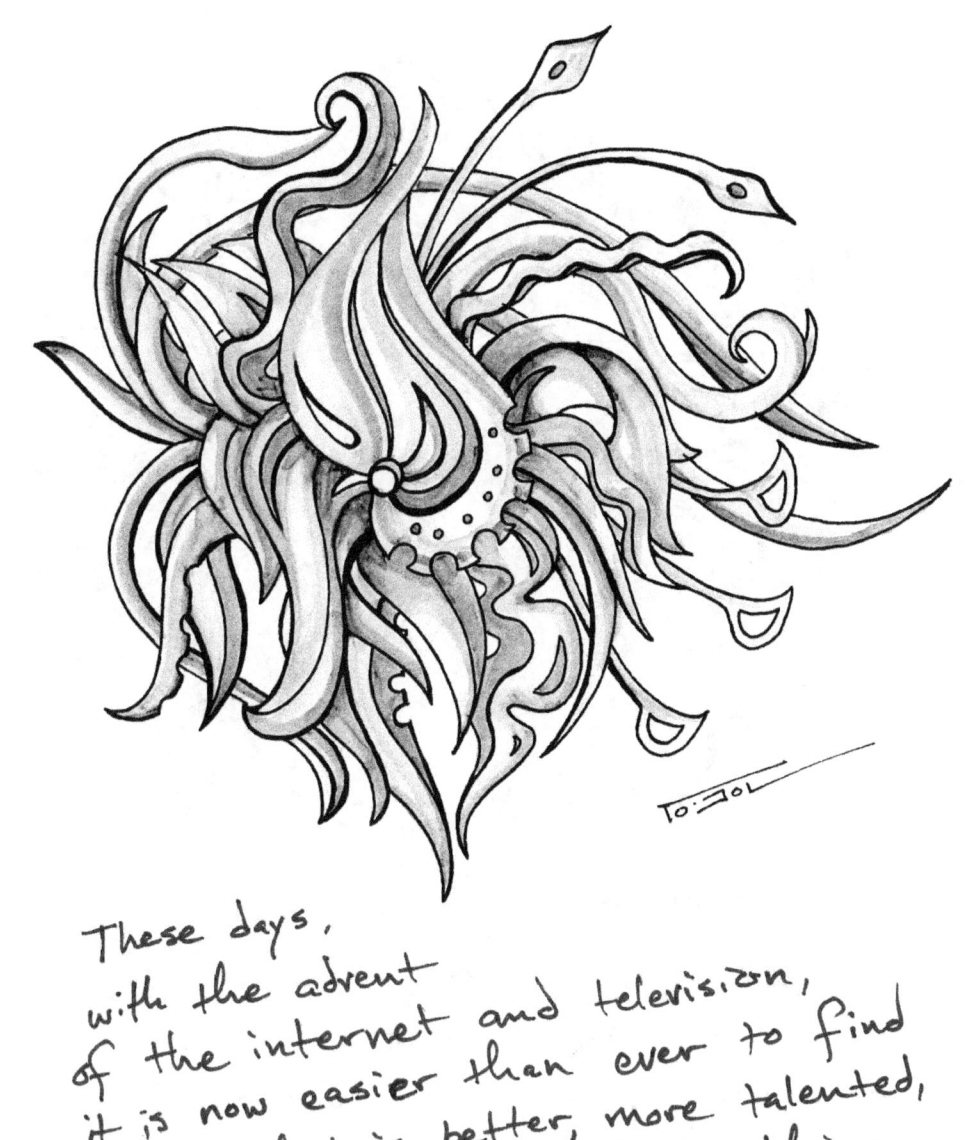

These days,
with the advent
of the internet and television,
it is now easier than ever to find
someone that is better, more talented,
faster, luckier, stronger, or anything
else. The only thing all these people
have in common is that they all
managed to ignore that crushing
perspective. They didn't give up.

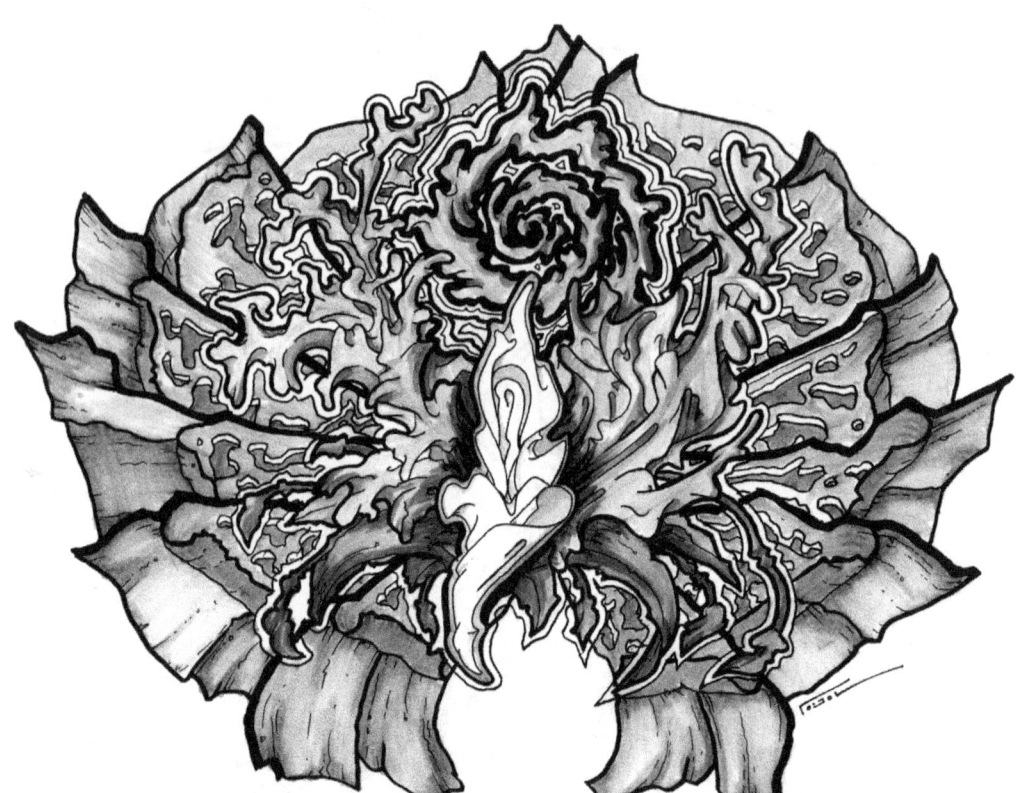

Keep moving forward. Every day, try
to take another step. Even if you
don't know where you're going. If
you're walking through a storm, don't
stop. Don't turn around if there's
a storm in the distance, it could
blow over before you get there.
Put your eyes on the next mile-
marker, and just head toward it.

Don't Stop.

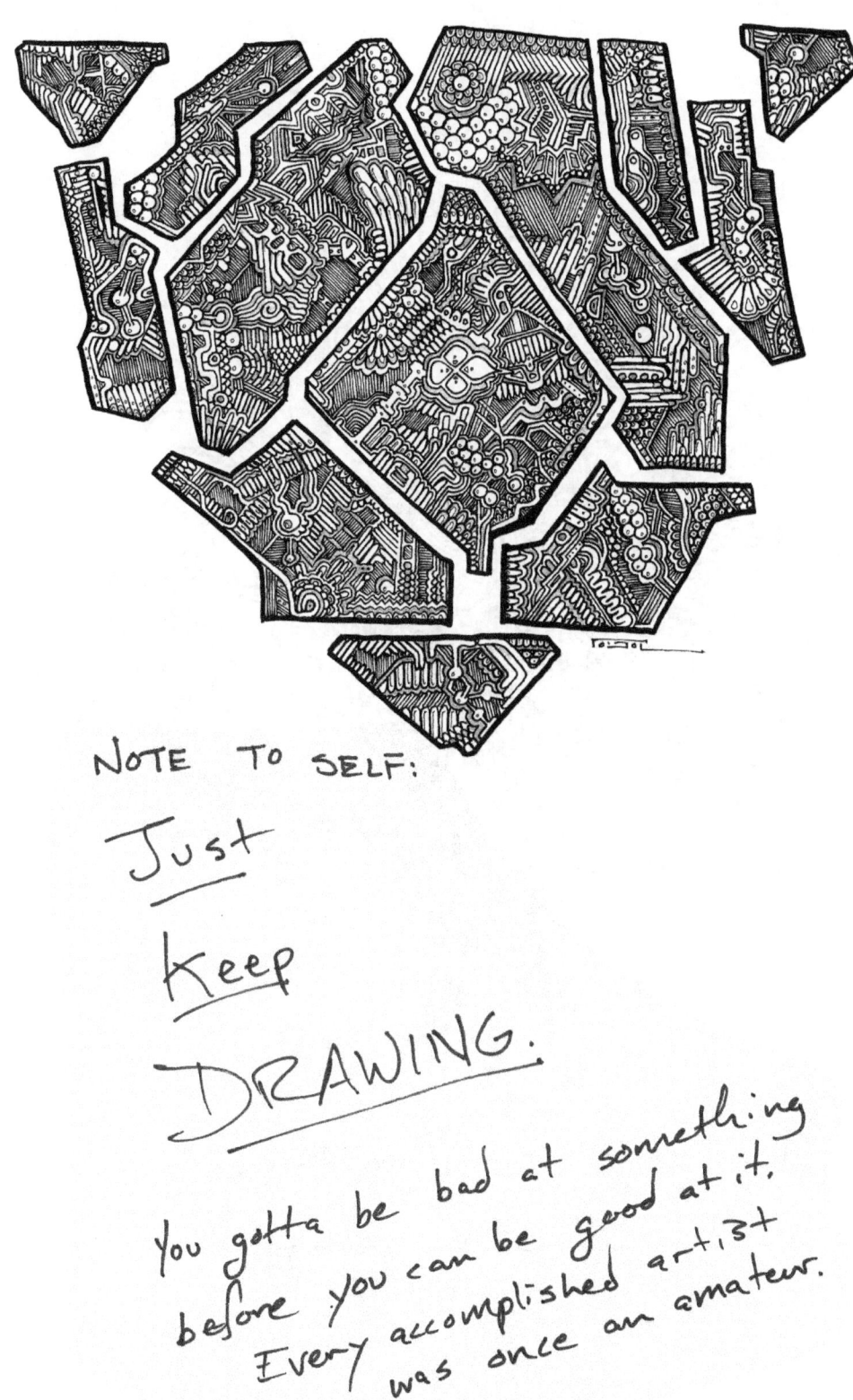

NOTE TO SELF:

Just

Keep

DRAWING.

You gotta be bad at something
before you can be good at it.
Every accomplished artist
was once an amateur.

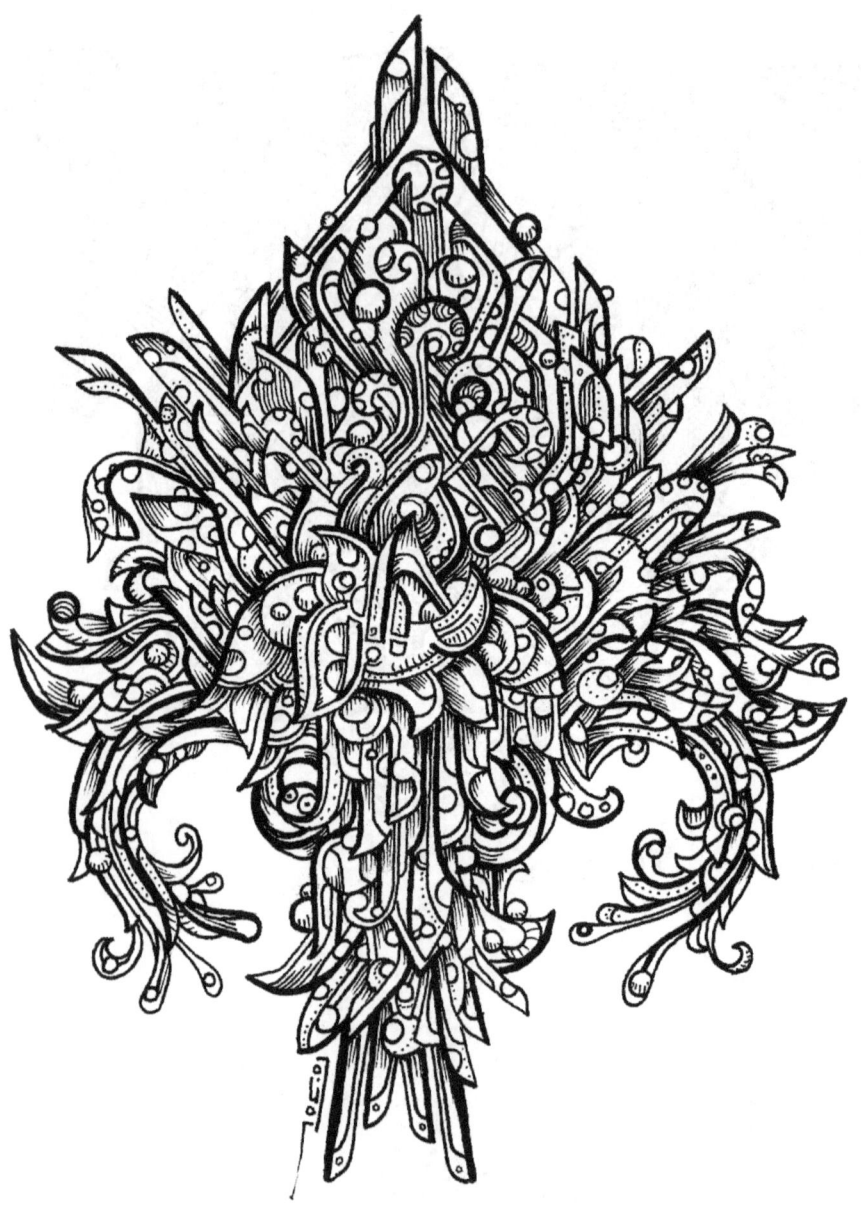

I like lines. More than
a lot of other things.

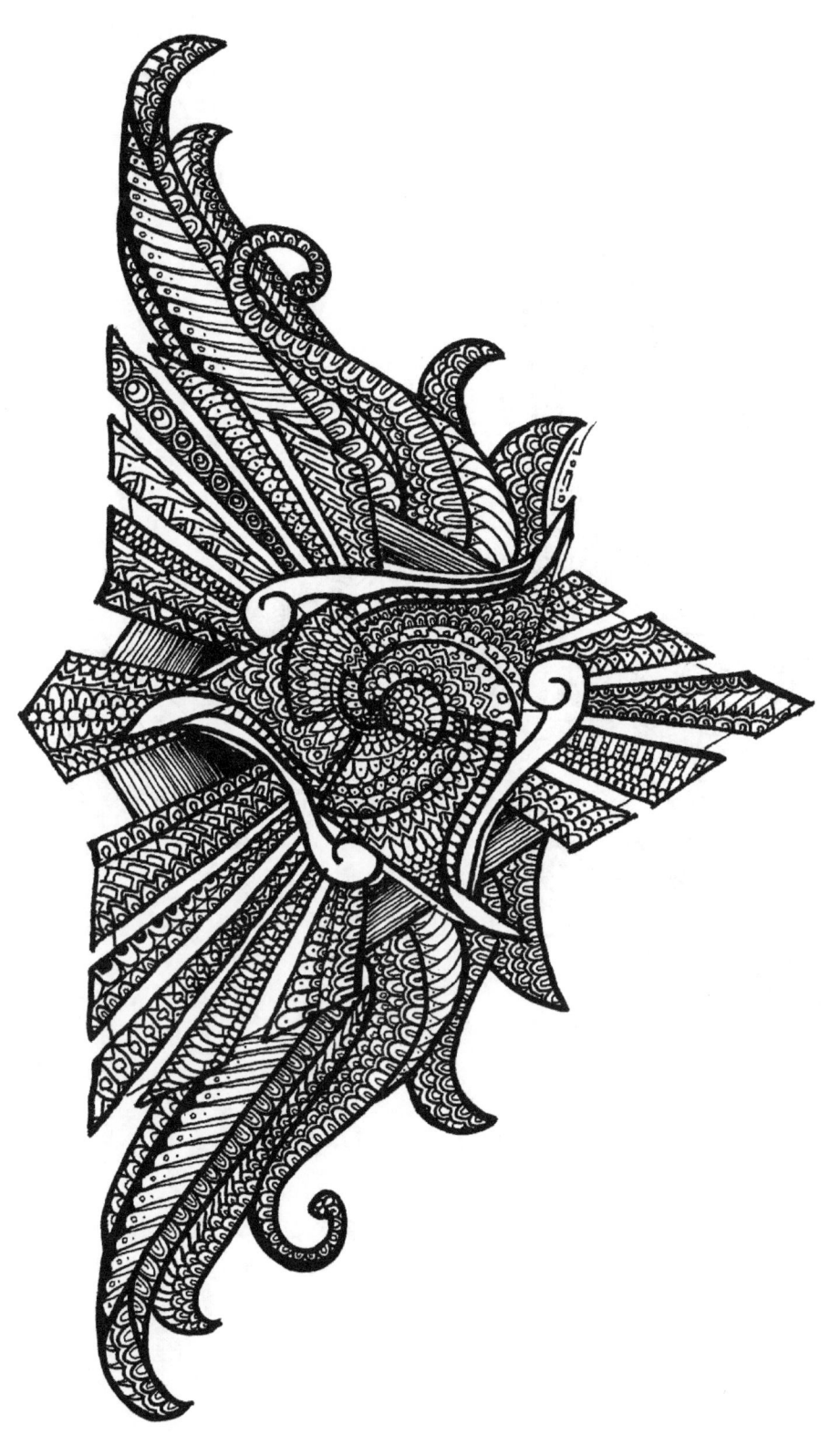

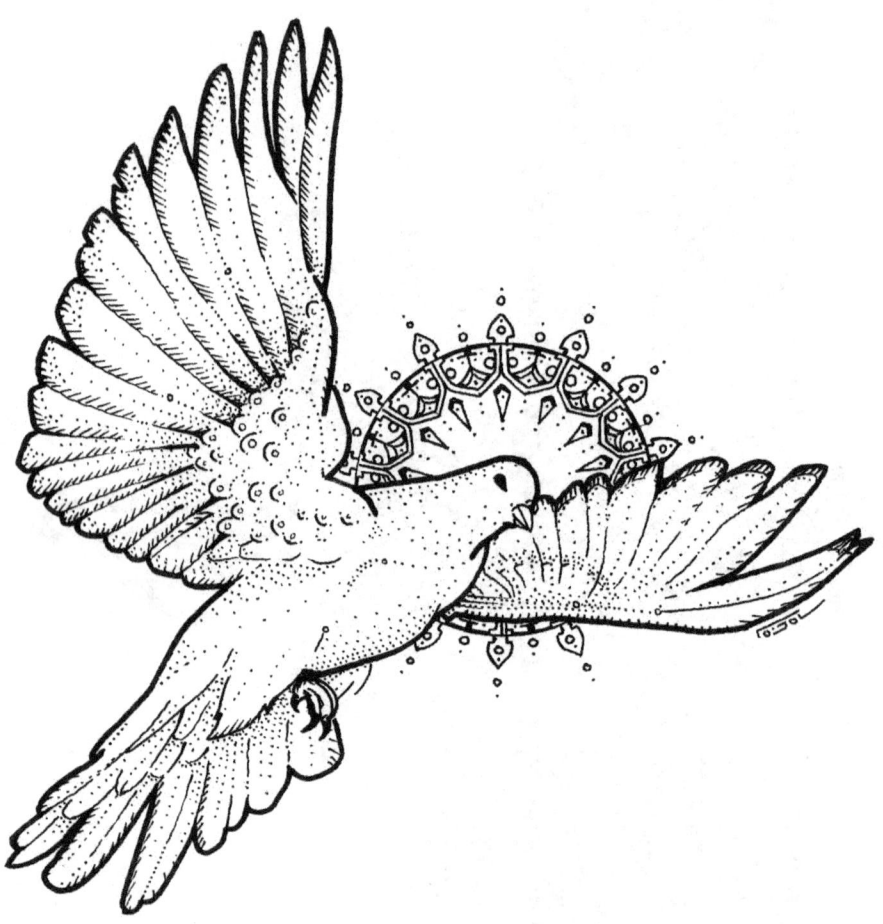

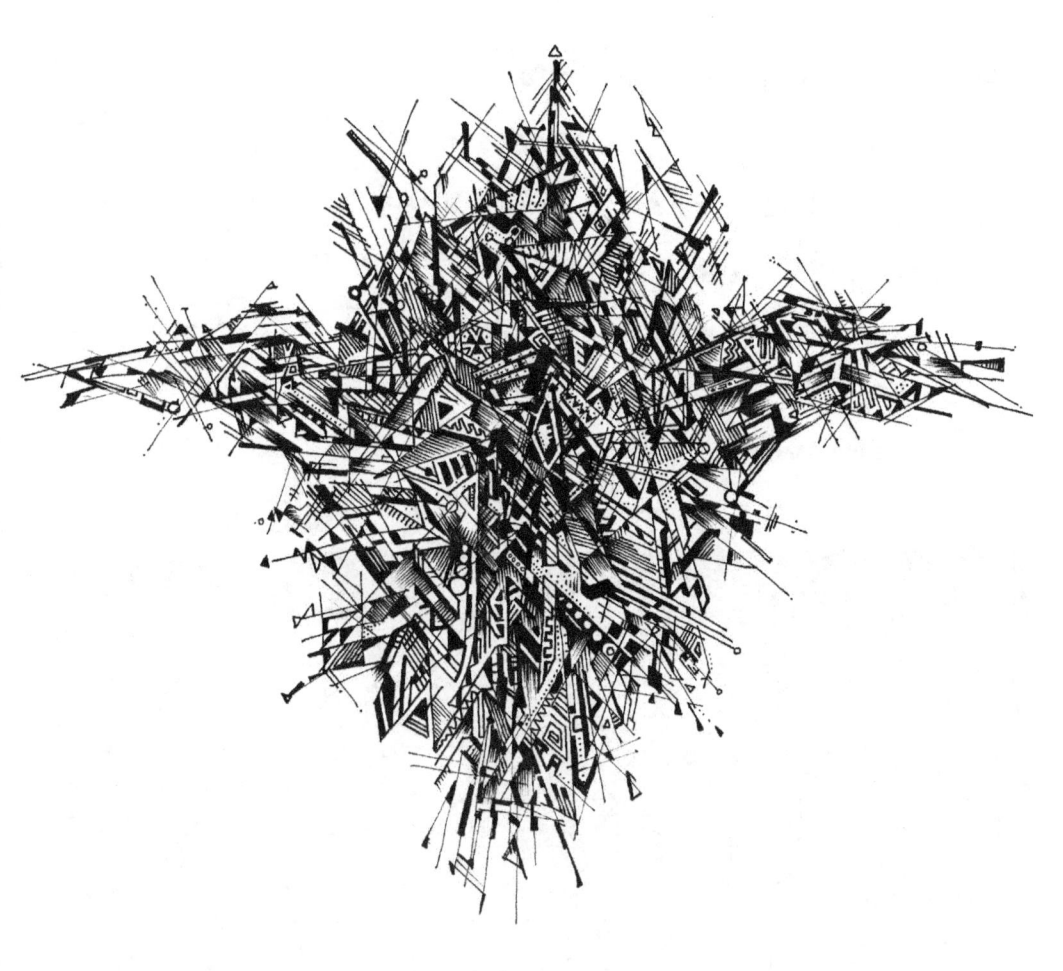

I like lines because they only do what I tell them to .... and I never have to tell them more than once. Unlike most things in my life, I have complete control.

But that also means that while I get all the credit for what I do with them, I also have to take all the blame. Sometimes, when I'm frustrated, I try to blame them, but then I remember they're...

JUST   LINES

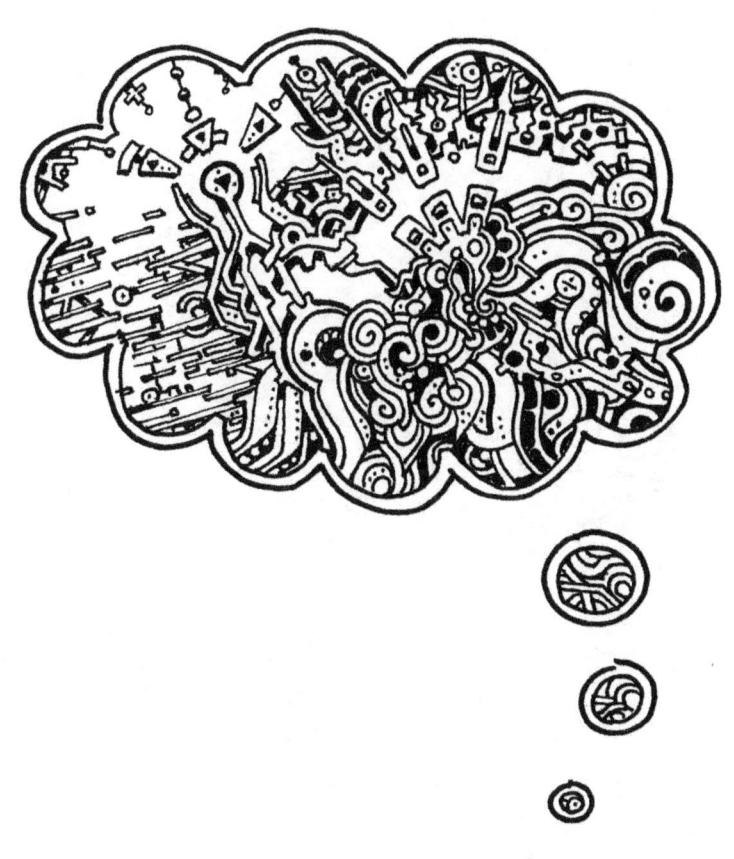

line of thought

Hand practice.

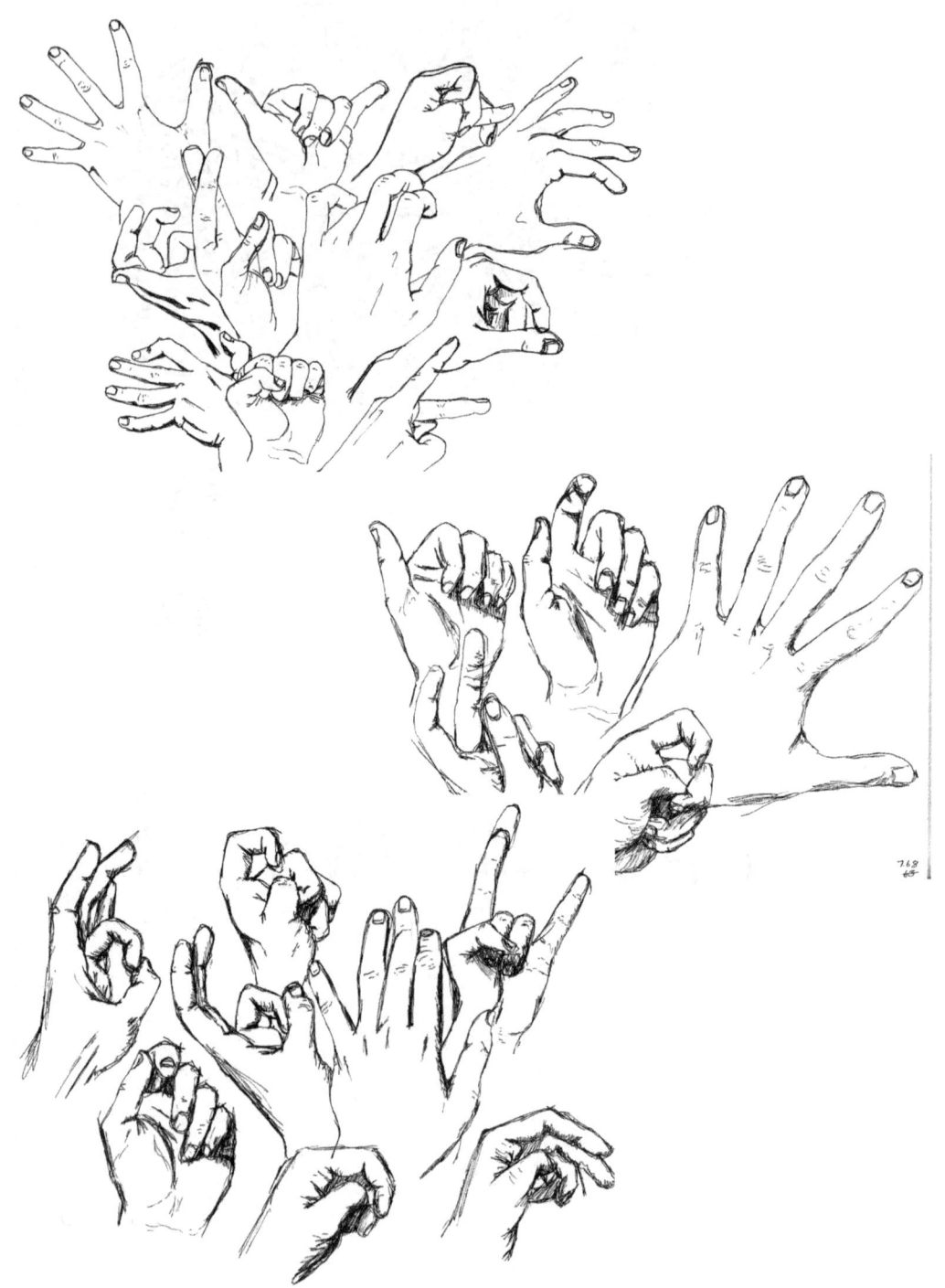

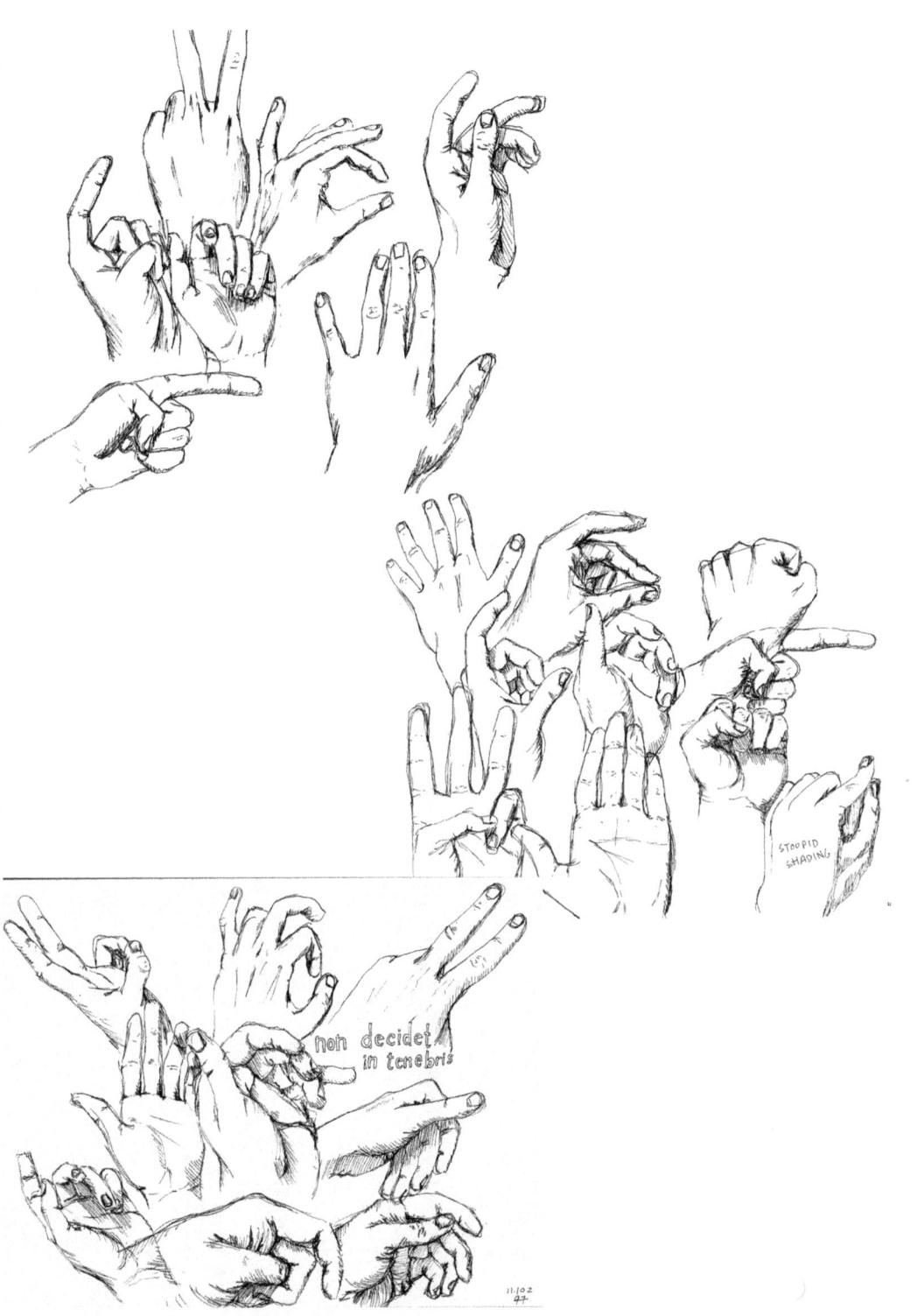

STOOPID SHADING

non decidet in tenebris

11.02
07

www.ingramcontent.com/pod-product-compliance
Lightning Source LLC
Chambersburg PA
CBHW071622170526
45166CB00003B/1161